Soups

Soups

Bounty
BOOKS

Part of the **MYRiAD** series

First published in Great Britain in 2004 by Hamlyn,
a division of Octopus Publishing Group Ltd

This edition published in 2011 by Bounty Books,
a division of Octopus Publishing Group Ltd
Endeavour House, 189 Shaftesbury Avenue,
London WC2H 8JY
www.octopusbooks.co.uk

An Hachette UK Company
www.hachette.co.uk

ISBN: 978-0-753722-61-9

A CIP catalogue record for this book is available
from the British Library

Printed and bound in China

Notes

Both metric and imperial measurements
are given for the recipes. Use one set of
measures only, not a mixture of both.

Ovens should be preheated to the
specified temperature. If using a fan-
assisted oven, follow the manufacturer's
instructions for adjusting the time
and temperature. Grills should also
be preheated.

This book includes dishes made with
nuts and nut derivatives. It is advisable
for those with known allergic reactions to
nuts and nut derivatives and those who
may be potentially vulnerable to these
allergies, such as pregnant and nursing
mothers, invalids, the elderly, babies and
children, to avoid dishes made with nuts
and nut oils. It is also prudent to check
the labels of preprepared ingredients for
the possible inclusion of nut derivatives.

Fresh herbs should be used unless
otherwise stated. If unavailable use dried
herbs as an alternative but halve the
quantities stated.

Contents

Introduction 6

Stock recipes 8

Quick and easy soups 12

Classic soups 32

Summer soups 52

Hot and spicy soups 76

Winter warmers 100

Index 126
Acknowledgements 128

Introduction

Piping hot, cool and chilled, light and healthy, hearty and nutritious, rich and creamy or sumptuous and sophisticated — soup comes in a thousand different forms. But there's one thing that every bowl of soup has in common — it's always a treat. Whether you're looking for the perfect comfort food or the ultimate health-kick, you will always find it in a bowl of soup.

A quick history

Soup has been eaten for millennia, ever since early man first discovered how to make vessels in which to boil food. The earliest soups were probably a by-product of cooking other foods in liquid — but since nothing was wasted in those times, the cooking broth was eaten too.

Today, every nation has their own soups — sup, zuppe, shorba, sopa, pho to name but a few. In Greece they eat egg and lemon Avgolemono; in Southeast Asia they enjoy fiery, fragrant broths, and creamy concoctions made with coconut milk. In Morocco the national soup is Harira, made of beans and lentils, which is favoured during the month-long fast of Ramadan. In Russia it is Borscht — served chunky or smooth, hot or cold, but always a vibrant purplish-red.

Classic soups are constantly evolving, being re-invented each time different cultures and cuisines collide. Mulligatawny was adopted and adapted by the British stationed in India during colonial times, while many Vietnamese soups show a distinct French influence. Modern chefs love to take old recipes such as Venetian Risi e Bisi and Hungarian Goulash and transform them into new and utterly delicious soups.

Getting started

Soups are one of the easiest dishes to make and all the recipes in this book are simple to prepare and cook. All you need is a chopping board and knife, a large saucepan for cooking and a wooden spoon for stirring. If the soup needs to be blended, a blender or food processor is invaluable. However, many soups can be puréed using a mouli or food mill, and coarse-textured vegetable soups can often be achieved simply by using a potato masher.

Perfect results

The key to a good soup is using good-quality ingredients, and the most important ingredient of all is stock. Stock forms the base of almost every soup, and it is upon this that all the other flavours build. A poor-quality stock can spoil a soup, no matter how delicious the other ingredients are. It is best to use fresh, homemade stock (see recipes on pages 8–11). However, you can also buy excellent fresh stocks in supermarkets. Stock cubes and stock powders make a good storecupboard standby, but buy a good-quality brand as the flavour can vary enormously.

Time-savers

• Fresh stock can be stored in the freezer, so it's well worth keeping a batch at the ready. Make a large amount and freeze in several smaller containers so that you can defrost one quantity at a time.

• Another great time-saver is using canned pulses instead of dried. If using pulses in brine, rinse well and taste the soup before adding extra salt.

• When buying meat, fish or shellfish, ask for it to be prepared for you ready for cooking, where possible.

Freezing soups

It can be useful to make a double batch of soup and freeze half for another day. As a general rule, smooth and chunky vegetable soups freeze well. Delicate broths containing tofu and noodles, and soups containing shellfish and eggs, will not freeze successfully. To freeze soups containing cream and cheese, it is best to freeze the soup before these ingredients are added; stir them into the soup once it has been defrosted and reheated. Fresh herbs and garnishes should always be added at the last minute, never frozen in the soup.

The finishing touch

When it comes to serving soup, presentation is everything. The same bowl of tomato soup can make a comforting meal when you're ill, a hearty and nutritious supper on a cold winter evening or a stunning dish for entertaining, depending on how you present it. For convalescence, serve it plain and piping hot; for sustenance, scatter over strips of frazzled bacon and grated cheese and serve with chunks of crusty bread; and for sophistication, ladle the soup into elegant soup plates, add a swirl of cream and scatter over fresh basil leaves.

Soups can be garnished in a hundred different ways. Simplest of all are fresh herbs; go for classic flavour combinations such as carrot and coriander, or spinach and dill. Spices such as paprika can make a good garnish too. Dress up Asian-style soups with shreds of spring onion and fiery chilli, or top Mediterranean-style soups with shavings of Parmesan cheese. Crunchy fried shallots, colourful vegetable crisps or tortilla chips make a great alternative to the classic croûton, and a spoonful of tangy salsa or fragrant pesto can make a sensational change to the traditional dollop of cream. When you're choosing a garnish, the golden rule is be creative and, above all, have fun!

Vegetable stock

makes **about 1.8 litres (3 pints)**
preparation time **15 minutes**
cooking time **2½–3 hours**

1.8 litres (3 pints) water
1 onion, unpeeled and halved
1 garlic clove, unpeeled and halved
1 carrot, roughly chopped
1 celery stick with leaves, roughly
    chopped
¼ small swede, unpeeled and
    roughly chopped
1 leek, white and green parts,
    roughly chopped
1 parsley sprig
6 black peppercorns
1 bay leaf
1 bouquet garni
peelings of 1–2 scrubbed potatoes
outer leaves of cauliflower,
    cabbage, Brussels sprouts
    (optional)
salt

1 Combine the measured water with all the remaining ingredients in a deep saucepan. Bring to the boil, then lower the heat and simmer, covered, for 2½–3 hours. Skim off the scum with a slotted spoon from time to time.

2 Cool, then strain through a sieve, discarding all the vegetables and herbs in the sieve. Cover the stock closely and store in the refrigerator. Use within 3–4 days. This stock is suitable for freezing; if frozen, use within 4 months.

Chicken stock

makes **3.6 litres (6 pints)**
preparation time **5–8 minutes**
cooking time **2½–3 hours**

1 whole chicken carcass
3.6 litres (6 pints) water
1 teaspoon salt
1 Spanish onion, peeled and stuck
   with 4 cloves
2 celery sticks, chopped
2 carrots, roughly chopped
2 parsley sprigs
1 bouquet garni
1 bay leaf
8 black peppercorns

1 Put the carcass into a deep saucepan, cover with the measured water and add the salt. Bring to the boil, skimming off the scum with a slotted spoon. Lower the heat, partially cover the pan and simmer for 1 hour.

2 Add the onion, celery, carrots, parsley, bouquet garni, bay leaf and peppercorns. Stir and continue simmering, partially covered, for a further 1½–2 hours. Add more water if the level drops below the bones.

3 Cool slightly. Remove the carcass, then strain the stock through a fine sieve into a bowl, discarding all the vegetables and herbs. After straining the stock, pick over the carcass, remove any meat still on the bones and add it to the stock.

4 Leave to cool, then skim off the fat with a spoon or blot with kitchen paper. Cover the stock closely and store in the refrigerator. Use within 3 days. This stock is suitable for freezing; if frozen, use within 3 months.

Fish stock

makes **1 litre (1¾ pints)**
preparation time **5–8 minutes**
cooking time **30–40 minutes**

500 g (1 lb) fish trimmings (bones,
   heads, tails, skins)
900 ml (1½ pints) water
1 onion, quartered
2 celery sticks with leaves,
   roughly chopped
1 bay leaf
1 parsley sprig
¼ teaspoon salt
6 black peppercorns
150 ml (¼ pint) dry white wine
   or cider

1 Put the fish trimmings into a large saucepan and cover with the measured water. Add all the remaining ingredients, stir well and bring to the boil, skimming off the scum as it rises to the surface with a slotted spoon. Lower the heat and simmer, partially covered, for 30–40 minutes.

2 Remove the saucepan from the heat and strain the mixture through a sieve, discarding the fish trimmings and other ingredients. Cool, then cover closely and store in the refrigerator. Use within 2 days. This stock is suitable for freezing; if frozen, use within 2 months.

tip The heads, tails and bones of white fish, such as cod, haddock, plaice, hake or whiting, make a good stock, but oily fish like mackerel and herring are not suitable.

Beef stock

makes **3.6 litres (6 pints)**
preparation time **15 minutes**
cooking time **about 4 hours**

about 1 kg (2 lb) marrow and
   skin bones
3.6 litres (6 pints) water
1 teaspoon salt
1 onion, quartered
2 celery sticks with leaves,
   roughly chopped
2 carrots, roughly chopped
4 parsley sprigs
1 bouquet garni
8 black peppercorns

1 Put the bones into a large saucepan. Cover them with the measured water and add the salt. Bring the liquid to the boil, skimming off any scum that rises to the surface with a slotted spoon. Lower the heat, partially cover the pan and simmer over a low heat for 2 hours. Skim from time to time.

2 Add the remaining ingredients and continue to simmer for a further 2 hours. Add more water if the level drops below the bones.

3 Cool slightly, then strain the stock through a fine sieve into a bowl, discarding the bones, vegetables, herbs and spices. Leave the stock to cool, then skim off the fat with a spoon or blot with kitchen paper. Cover the stock closely and store in the refrigerator. Use within 3 days. This stock is suitable for freezing; if frozen, use within 3 months.

Quick and Easy Soups

Simple, healthy and requiring minimal time in the kitchen, these soups are the ultimate convenience food. The recipes in this chapter are ideal for light lunches, afterwork snacks or impromptu meals for unexpected visitors.

Broccoli and cheese soup

serves **6**
preparation time **20 minutes**
cooking time **35–40 minutes**

1 kg (2 lb) broccoli
50 g (2 oz) butter
1 onion, chopped
1 large potato, peeled and
    quartered
1.5 litres (2$\frac{1}{2}$ pints) Vegetable
    Stock (see page 8)
125 ml (4 fl oz) single cream
1 tablespoon lemon juice
1 teaspoon Worcestershire sauce
a few drops of Tabasco sauce,
    or to taste
125 g (4 oz) mature Cheddar,
    grated
salt and pepper
watercress sprigs, to garnish

1 Remove all the tough stems and leaves from the broccoli. Cut off the stalks, peel them and cut them into 2.5 cm (1 inch) pieces. Break the florets into very small pieces and set them aside.

2 Melt the butter in a large saucepan. Add the onion and broccoli stalks and cook, covered, for 5 minutes over a moderate heat, stirring frequently.

3 Add the reserved broccoli florets, potato and stock to the pan. Bring the mixture to the boil. Cook, partially covered, for 5 minutes. Season the mixture to taste with salt and pepper and continue to cook over a moderate heat for 20 minutes, or until all the vegetables are soft.

4 Using a blender or food processor, purée the mixture until smooth, then transfer to a clean saucepan. Add the cream, lemon juice, Worcestershire sauce and Tabasco to the pan. Simmer for 3–5 minutes. Do not allow to boil or the soup will curdle. Just before serving, stir in the grated cheese and garnish each portion with watercress sprigs.

Parsnip and fennel soup

serves **4–6**
preparation time **10–15 minutes**
cooking time **35–40 minutes**

50 g (2 oz) butter
500 g (1 lb) parsnips, cut into
   5 mm (¼ inch) dice
500 g (1 lb) fennel bulb, cut into
   small pieces of equal size
1 onion, chopped
3 tablespoons cornflour
1.2 litres (2 pints) hot Vegetable
   or Chicken Stock (see pages 8
   and 9)
150 ml (¼ pint) double cream
salt and pepper

1 Melt the butter in a large saucepan. Add the parsnips, fennel and onion and cook over a moderate heat for 15 minutes, or until the vegetables are soft, stirring constantly.

2 In a small bowl, mix the cornflour with 150 ml (¼ pint) of the hot stock until thick and smooth. Fold the mixture into the vegetables, then pour in the remaining hot stock, stirring the soup constantly.

3 Bring the mixture to the boil, then lower the heat and simmer, partially covered, for 20 minutes, stirring frequently. Add salt and pepper to taste, stir in the cream and heat through without boiling. Serve at once in warmed soup bowls.

Carrot and ginger soup

serves **4**
preparation time **20 minutes**
cooking time **25–30 minutes**

2 tablespoons olive oil
1 large onion, chopped
1–2 garlic cloves, crushed
1 tablespoon finely grated fresh
   root ginger
375 g (12 oz) carrots, sliced
900 ml (1½ pints) Vegetable or
   Chicken Stock (see pages 8
   and 9)
2 tablespoons lime or lemon juice
salt and pepper

To serve
soured cream
2 spring onions, finely chopped

1 Heat the oil in a saucepan over a low heat, add the onion, garlic and ginger and cook for 5–6 minutes, or until softened.

2 Add the carrots and stock and bring to the boil, then reduce the heat and simmer for 15–20 minutes, or until the carrots are tender.

3 Purée the soup in a blender or food processor with the lime or lemon juice until smooth. Strain it through a sieve and return to the saucepan to reheat. Serve with a spoonful of soured cream in each bowl of soup and sprinkle with spring onions.

Potato soup with parsley

serves **4**
preparation time **10 minutes**
cooking time **20 minutes**

1.5 litres (2¹/₂ pints) Beef Stock
   (see page 11)
4 potatoes, coarsely grated
1 egg yolk
1 hard-boiled egg yolk, mashed
50 ml (2 fl oz) single cream
50 g (2 oz) grated Parmesan
   cheese
1 tablespoon finely chopped
   parsley
salt and pepper
125 g (4 oz) croûtons, to serve
   (see below)

1 Put the stock into a saucepan and bring to the boil. Sprinkle the potatoes with salt and pepper to taste, then drop them into the boiling stock. Cook for about 15 minutes, stirring from time to time.

2 Beat the egg yolk in a soup tureen and add the mashed hard-boiled egg yolk. Blend the cream, Parmesan and parsley into the egg mixture and whisk them together.

3 Carefully pour 250 ml (8 fl oz) of the stock into the egg mixture. Reheat the remaining stock and potatoes and gradually add them to the soup tureen. Sprinkle with croûtons and serve in warmed soup bowls.

tip To make croûtons, cut the crusts off 2 slices of white bread, then cube the bread. Heat 1 tablespoon vegetable oil in a heavy-based frying pan and fry the bread cubes, turning and stirring frequently, for 1–2 minutes, or until golden and crisp.

Courgette and mint soup

serves **4**
preparation time **20 minutes**
cooking time **20–25 minutes**

50 g (2 oz) butter
1 small onion, chopped
1–2 garlic cloves, crushed
750 g (1½ lb) courgettes, diced
finely grated rind of 1 lemon
600 ml (1 pint) Vegetable or
    Chicken Stock (see pages 8
    and 9), or water
2–3 tablespoons chopped mint
2 egg yolks
100 ml (3½ fl oz) double cream
salt and pepper
single cream, to garnish

1 Melt the butter in a saucepan over a low heat, add the onion and garlic and cook for 5–6 minutes, or until softened. Stir in the courgettes and lemon rind and cook for a further 5–10 minutes, or until tender. Add the stock or water and mint and bring to the boil, then lower the heat and simmer for 5 minutes.

2 Purée the soup in a blender or food processor until smooth, then strain through a sieve.

3 Immediately before serving, reheat the soup to just below boiling point. Mix together the egg yolks and double cream in a small bowl and whisk in a ladleful of the hot soup. Whisk this mixture back into the pan; do not allow the soup to boil or it will curdle. Season to taste with salt and pepper and serve in warmed soup bowls. Drizzle with single cream before serving.

Pea, lettuce and lemon soup with sesame croûtons

serves **4**
preparation time **10 minutes**
cooking time **20 minutes**

25 g (1 oz) butter
1 large onion, finely chopped
425 g (14 oz) frozen peas
2 Little Gem lettuces, roughly
   chopped
1 litre (1³/₄ pints) Vegetable or
   Chicken Stock (see pages 8
   and 9)
grated rind and juice of ¹/₂ lemon
salt and pepper

Sesame croûtons
2 thick slices of bread, cubed
1 tablespoon olive oil
1 tablespoon sesame seeds

1 To make the sesame croûtons, brush the bread cubes with the oil and place in a roasting tin. Sprinkle with the sesame seeds and cook in a preheated oven at 200°C (400°F), Gas Mark 6, for 10–15 minutes, or until golden.

2 Meanwhile, heat the butter in a large saucepan, add the onion and cook for 5 minutes, or until beginning to soften. Add the peas, lettuce, stock, lemon rind and juice and seasoning. Bring to the boil, then reduce the heat, cover and simmer for 10–15 minutes.

3 Allow the soup to cool slightly, then transfer to a blender or food processor and purée until smooth. Return the soup to the pan, adjust the seasoning if necessary and heat through. Spoon into warmed soup bowls and sprinkle with the sesame croûtons.

Spinach and broccoli soup

serves **4**
preparation time **10 minutes**
cooking time **20 minutes**

2 tablespoons olive oil
50 g (2 oz) butter
1 onion, diced
1 garlic clove, finely chopped
2 potatoes, diced
250 g (8 oz) broccoli, chopped
300 g (10 oz) spinach, chopped
900 ml (1½ pints) Vegetable or
   Chicken Stock (see pages 8
   and 9)
125 g (4 oz) Gorgonzola cheese,
   crumbled into small pieces
juice of ½ lemon
½ teaspoon grated nutmeg
salt and pepper
75 g (3 oz) toasted pine nuts,
   to garnish
warm crusty bread, to serve

1 Heat the oil and butter in a saucepan, add the onion and garlic and cook for 3 minutes. Add the potatoes, broccoli, spinach and stock and bring to the boil, then lower the heat and simmer for 15 minutes.

2 Add the Gorgonzola to the soup with the lemon juice, nutmeg and salt and pepper to taste. For a smooth consistency, purée the soup in a blender or food processor. Alternatively, it can be left with chunky pieces according to taste. Spoon into warmed soup bowls, garnish with toasted pine nuts and serve with warm crusty bread.

Watercress soup with poached quails' eggs

serves **4**
preparation time **5 minutes**
cooking time **20–25 minutes**

50 g (2 oz) butter
1 onion, finely chopped
250 g (8 oz) potatoes, cut into
    1 cm (½ inch) cubes
300 g (10 oz) watercress, roughly
    chopped
900 ml (1½ pints) Vegetable or
    Chicken Stock (see pages 8
    and 9)
300 ml (½ pint) single cream
12 quails' eggs
salt and pepper
50 g (2 oz) Parmesan cheese, finely
    grated, to serve

1 Melt the butter in a large saucepan, add the onion and cook gently, without allowing it to colour, for 8–10 minutes, or until well softened. Stir in the potatoes and watercress, cover and cook for 3–5 minutes, stirring once or twice, until the watercress has just wilted.

2 Add the stock and season with salt and pepper. Bring to the boil, then lower the heat and simmer for 6–8 minutes, or until the potatoes are tender.

3 Purée the soup in a blender or food processor until smooth. Strain it through a sieve and return to the pan. Add the cream, adjust the seasoning to taste and heat through without boiling.

4 Poach the quails' eggs in a saucepan of gently simmering water. Remove the eggs with a slotted spoon and drain well on kitchen paper. Place 3 eggs in each serving bowl. Ladle the watercress soup over the eggs and serve with the grated Parmesan.

Avgolemono

serves **4–6**

preparation time **about**
10 minutes

cooking time **25 minutes**

1.5 litres (2½ pints) Vegetable or
   Chicken Stock (see pages 8
   and 9)
50 g (2 oz) long-grain white rice
2 eggs
2–3 tablespoons lemon juice
salt and pepper
1 tablespoon chopped parsley,
   to garnish (optional)

1 Combine the stock, ½ teaspoon of salt and the rice
in a saucepan. Bring the mixture to the boil. Stir, then
lower the heat, cover and simmer for 20 minutes. Stir
once more.

2 Beat the eggs in a small bowl, then whisk in the
lemon juice. Add a ladleful of stock, beat, then add
another ladleful of stock and beat again.

3 Bring the remaining stock and rice mixture to the
boil. Briefly remove the saucepan from the heat and
add the egg and lemon mixture. Stir well, lower the
heat and simmer for a further 2 minutes, then add salt
and pepper to taste. Sprinkle on the parsley, if liked.
Serve immediately in warmed soup bowls.

Crab soup

serves **4–6**
preparation time **10 minutes**
cooking time **about 20 minutes**

1 litre (1³/₄ pints) Chicken Stock
  (see page 9)
2.5 cm (1 inch) piece of fresh root
  ginger, peeled and very finely
  chopped
2 ripe tomatoes, skinned, deseeded
  and very finely chopped
¹/₂ small red or green chilli,
  deseeded and very finely
  chopped
2 tablespoons rice wine or
  dry sherry
1 tablespoon rice wine vinegar or
  white wine or cider vinegar
¹/₂ teaspoon sugar
1 tablespoon cornflour
about 150 g (5 oz) white crab
  meat, defrosted and drained
  thoroughly if frozen
salt and pepper
2 spring onions, finely sliced
  lengthways, to garnish

1 Put the stock into a large saucepan with the ginger, tomatoes, chilli, rice wine or sherry, vinegar and sugar. Bring to the boil, then cover, lower the heat and simmer for about 10 minutes to allow the flavours to mingle and mellow.

2 Blend the cornflour to a paste with a little cold water, then pour it into the soup and stir to mix. Simmer, stirring, for 1–2 minutes, or until the soup thickens.

3 Add the crab meat, stir gently to mix, then heat through for 2–3 minutes. Taste and add salt and pepper if necessary. Serve piping hot in warmed soup bowls, sprinkled with the sliced spring onions.

tip Frozen white crab meat is convenient to use and it can be found in large supermarkets. Alternatively, you can buy a whole cooked fresh crab from a fishmonger and have the meat removed for you.

Chicken and coconut milk soup

serves **4**
preparation time **6 minutes**
cooking time **10 minutes**

300 ml (½ pint) Chicken Stock
  (see page 9)
3 Kaffir lime leaves, torn
½ lemon grass stalk, obliquely
  sliced
2.5 cm (1 inch) piece of galangal,
  peeled and finely sliced
100 ml (3½ fl oz) coconut milk
4 tablespoons Thai fish sauce
1 teaspoon palm sugar or light
  muscovado sugar
3 tablespoons lime juice
125 g (4 oz) chicken, skinned and
  cut into bite-sized pieces
2 tablespoons chilli oil or 2 small
  chillies, finely sliced (optional)

1 Heat the stock in a saucepan, then stir in the lime leaves, lemon grass and galangal. As the stock is simmering, add the coconut milk, fish sauce, sugar and lime juice and stir well.

2 Add the chicken and simmer for 5 minutes.

3 Just before serving, add the chilli oil or chillies, if liked, stir again and serve in warmed soup bowls.

Pork ball and tofu soup

serves **4**
preparation time **10 minutes**
cooking time **12–13 minutes**

600 ml (1 pint) Chicken Stock
  (see page 9)
1 garlic clove, finely chopped
4 garlic cloves, halved
$\frac{1}{2}$ teaspoon ground black pepper
8 fresh coriander roots
200 g (7 oz) silken tofu, cut into
  2.5 cm (1 inch) slices
1 sheet roasted laver seaweed,
  torn into shreds
2 tablespoons light soy sauce
fresh coriander leaves, to garnish

Pork balls
65 g (2$\frac{1}{2}$ oz) minced pork
1 tablespoon light soy sauce
$\frac{1}{2}$ teaspoon ground black pepper

1 Heat the stock with the chopped and halved garlic, pepper and coriander in a saucepan. While the soup is heating, make the pork balls.

2 Mix together the pork, soy sauce and pepper, then form the mixture into small balls. Drop them into the soup and simmer gently for 6–7 minutes.

3 Add the tofu, laver and soy sauce, stir for 30 seconds, then serve the soup in warmed bowls, garnished with coriander leaves.

Prawn and lemon grass soup

serves **4**
preparation time **25 minutes**
cooking time **20 minutes**

375 g (12 oz) raw prawns
3 lemon grass stalks, cut into
    2.5 cm (1 inch) pieces
1.2 litres (2 pints) water
1 tomato, quartered and deseeded
475 g (15 oz) can straw
    mushrooms, drained
6 Kaffir lime leaves
1 spring onion, chopped
185 g (6½ oz) bean sprouts
juice of 3 limes
2 small red chillies, finely sliced
4 tablespoons Vietnamese or Thai
    fish sauce
salt and pepper
fresh coriander leaves, to garnish

1 Peel and devein the prawns and set aside the shells. Cut off the white part of the lemon grass stalks, reserving the tops. Flatten the lemon grass stalks with a cleaver or pestle.

2 Heat the measured water in a saucepan and add the prawn shells and the lemon grass tops. Bring the water slowly to the boil, strain and return to the saucepan. Add the flattened lemon grass, tomato, straw mushrooms and lime leaves. Bring back to the boil, then lower the heat to a simmer and cook for 3–4 minutes.

3 Add the prawns and, when they have changed colour, add the spring onion, bean sprouts, lime juice, chillies and fish sauce. Season to taste with salt and pepper and stir well.

4 Serve in individual warmed soup bowls, sprinkled with coriander leaves.

Classic Soups

Everyone has a favourite soup and these
recipes show you how to make them with
minimum fuss. From the creamy *Vichyssoise*
and the chunky *Minestrone*, to the spicy
Mulligatawny and the luxurious *Prawn Bisque*.

Tomato soup with croûtons

serves **4**
preparation time **10 minutes**
cooking time **40 minutes**

4 tablespoons olive oil
1 onion, chopped
3 garlic cloves, crushed
750 g (1½ lb) tomatoes, skinned
   and chopped
1 litre (1¾ pints) Vegetable or
   Chicken Stock (see pages 8
   and 9)
salt and pepper
croûtons, to serve (see page 18)
a few basil leaves, chopped,
   to garnish

1 Heat half the oil in a large saucepan, add the onion and garlic and cook gently for 4–6 minutes, or until golden but not brown. Add the tomatoes and cook for 5 minutes, then gradually stir in the stock. Add salt and pepper to taste, then simmer for 30 minutes.

2 Meanwhile, make the croûtons.

3 Add the croûtons and the basil to the soup and serve immediately in warmed soup bowls.

Pumpkin soup

serves **6**
preparation time **about**
10 minutes
cooking time **40–45 minutes**

50 g (2 oz) butter
750 g (1½ lb) pumpkin, skinned,
    deseeded and cut into
    large pieces
150 ml (¼ pint) warm water
¼ teaspoon grated nutmeg
pinch of dried thyme
1.5 litres (2½ pints) milk
50 g (2 oz) long-grain white rice
salt and pepper
croûtons, to garnish (see page 18)

1 Melt the butter in a large saucepan. Add the pumpkin, stir well and cook over a low to moderate heat for 10 minutes. Add the measured warm water, nutmeg, thyme and salt and pepper to taste. Cover and cook over a high heat until the pumpkin is soft.

2 Purée the pumpkin mixture in a blender or food processor, with a little of the milk if necessary, until smooth. Transfer to a clean saucepan.

3 Add the remaining milk and rice to the pumpkin purée in the pan. Stir well and cook, covered, for 30 minutes, or until the rice is tender, stirring from time to time. Serve the pumpkin soup in warmed bowls, garnished with croûtons.

Roasted pepper soup with black pepper cream

serves **4**
preparation time **20 minutes**
cooking time **about 1 hour**

6 large red or yellow peppers
4 leeks, white and pale green parts
   only, thinly sliced
3 tablespoons olive oil
750 ml (1¼ pints) Vegetable or
   Chicken Stock (see pages 8
   and 9)
2 teaspoons black peppercorns
75 ml (3 fl oz) mascarpone cheese
75 ml (3 fl oz) milk
salt and pepper
toasted crusty bread, to serve

1 Put the peppers into a large roasting tin and roast in a preheated oven, 240°C (475°F), Gas Mark 9, for 20–30 minutes, turning once, until they begin to char. Remove the peppers from the oven, put them into a polythene bag and close it tightly. Leave for 10 minutes to steam.

2 Put the leeks into a bowl of cold water to soak for 5 minutes.

3 Remove the peppers from the bag and peel off the skins, then pull out the stalks – the seeds should come with them. Halve the peppers, scrape out any remaining seeds and roughly chop the flesh. Swish the leeks around in the water to loosen any mud, then drain and rinse well.

4 Heat the oil in a large saucepan, add the leeks and cook gently for 10 minutes until soft but not coloured. Add the peppers, stock and a little salt and pepper. Bring the mixture to the boil, then lower the heat and simmer for 20 minutes.

5 Pound or grind the black peppercorns as finely as possible. Beat the mascarpone with the milk and pepper. Season with salt, cover and chill in the refrigerator until needed.

6 Purée the soup in a blender or food processor, then pass it through a sieve into the rinsed-out pan. Reheat, taste and adjust the seasoning if necessary. Serve the soup in warmed bowls with dollops of the pepper cream and slices of toasted crusty bread.

Vichyssoise

serves **6**
preparation time **15 minutes**,
plus chilling
cooking time **about 35–40 minutes**

50 g (2 oz) butter
1 kg (2 lb) leeks, white parts only, finely sliced
1 onion, chopped
1 litre (1³/₄ pints) Vegetable or Chicken Stock (see pages 8 and 9)
pinch of grated nutmeg
750 g (1¹/₂ lb) old potatoes, cubed
600 ml (1 pint) milk
300 ml (¹/₂ pint) single cream
150 ml (¹/₄ pint) double cream, chilled
salt and white pepper
2 tablespoons snipped fresh chives, to garnish

1 Melt the butter in a saucepan. Add the leeks and onion and cook over a moderate heat for 5 minutes, stirring constantly. Do not allow the vegetables to change colour.

2 Add the stock, nutmeg, potatoes and salt and pepper to taste. Bring the mixture to the boil, then lower the heat and cook, partially covered, for 25 minutes. Pour in the milk and simmer for a further 5–8 minutes. Cool slightly.

3 Purée the mixture in a blender or food processor until smooth, then rub it through a sieve into a bowl. Add the single cream, stir well and cover the bowl closely. Chill in the refrigerator for at least 3 hours.

4 Just before serving, swirl in the double cream and add more salt and pepper if required. Serve in chilled bowls, garnishing each portion with a generous sprinkling of snipped chives.

Leek and potato soup

serves **4–6**
preparation time **15 minutes**
cooking time **40 minutes**

25 g (1 oz) butter
2 large leeks, finely sliced
250 g (8 oz) potatoes, roughly
　diced
1 onion, roughly chopped
750 ml (1¼ pints) Vegetable or
　Chicken Stock (see pages 8
　and 9), or water
300 ml (½ pint) milk
salt and pepper
1 tablespoon snipped chives,
　to garnish

1 Melt the butter in a large saucepan, add the leeks, potatoes and onion and stir well to coat with the butter. Cover tightly with a piece of greaseproof paper and cook over a very gentle heat for about 15 minutes, or until the vegetables have softened, stirring frequently to prevent them from browning.

2 Add the stock or water and milk and season to taste with salt and pepper. Bring to the boil, then lower the heat and simmer gently for about 20 minutes, or until the vegetables are tender.

3 Purée the mixture in a blender or food processor until smooth, then transfer it to a clean saucepan.

4 Adjust the seasoning if necessary and heat until very hot, then pour the soup into warmed bowls. Garnish with chives and serve.

Mushroom soup with crispy bacon

serves **4–6**
preparation time **15 minutes**
cooking time **25–30 minutes**

50 g (2 oz) butter
1 onion, finely chopped
1 clove garlic, finely chopped
375 g (12 oz) mushrooms,
    thinly sliced
2 tablespoons plain flour
600 ml (1 pint) Chicken Stock
    (see page 9)
150 ml ($\frac{1}{4}$ pint) milk
1 tablespoon Manzanilla sherry
    (optional)
150 ml ($\frac{1}{4}$ pint) single cream
4 rindless bacon rashers, cooked
    until crisp and broken into
    small pieces
salt and pepper
chervil sprigs, to garnish

1 Melt the butter in a large saucepan, add the onion, garlic and mushrooms and cook until soft and beginning to colour. Sprinkle on the flour and stir to combine. Gradually pour on the stock and milk, stirring well to blend. Bring to the boil, then lower the heat and simmer for about 15–20 minutes.

2 Add salt and pepper to taste, along with the sherry, if using, and half the cream. Reheat the soup without boiling, then pour into warmed soup bowls. Whip the remaining cream until it is just holding its shape, then spoon a little on top of each bowl of soup. Sprinkle with the bacon pieces and garnish with chervil sprigs.

tip A mixture of cultivated and wild mushrooms gives the soup a very special flavour. For a smoother soup, purée it before adding the cream.

French onion soup

serves **6**
preparation time **10 minutes**
cooking time **about 35 minutes**

50 g (2 oz) butter
500 g (1 lb) Spanish onions, sliced
    into fairly thick rings
25 g (1 oz) plain flour
1.2 litres (2 pints) Vegetable or
    Beef Stock (see pages 8 and 11)
1 tablespoon Cognac (optional)
½ teaspoon Dijon mustard
salt and pepper

To garnish
6 slices of French bread
75 g (3 oz) Gruyère cheese, grated
finely chopped parsley

1 Melt the butter in a large saucepan, add the onions and cook over a moderate heat, stirring constantly, until soft and pale gold in colour. Sprinkle in the flour and stir for about 1 minute, then gradually pour in the stock. Bring the mixture to the boil, stirring constantly, and add salt and pepper to taste.

2 Lower the heat and simmer for 20–25 minutes. Stir in the Cognac, if using, and the mustard. Keep the soup hot.

3 Grill the bread for the garnish until it is lightly browned, then sprinkle each slice with the grated Gruyère. Pour the soup into heatproof bowls and float a slice of cheese-topped bread in each bowl. Put the bowls under a preheated grill until the cheese melts and bubbles. Sprinkle with chopped parsley and serve the soup immediately.

Ham and pea soup

serves **6**
preparation time **10 minutes**,
plus soaking
cooking time **1¼ hours**

250 g (8 oz) yellow or green split
    peas, soaked for 4–6 hours in
    cold water to cover
50 g (2 oz) butter
1 large onion, roughly chopped
1 large carrot, roughly chopped
4 thick bacon rashers,
    approximately 175 g (6 oz),
    derinded and diced
1 small bay leaf
1 ham bone
1.2 litres (2 pints) water
2 tablespoons snipped chives
salt and pepper

1 Drain the split peas in a colander and discard the soaking water.

2 Melt the butter in a saucepan, add the onion, carrot and two-thirds of the bacon and cook gently for about 15 minutes, or until soft. Add the drained split peas, bay leaf, ham bone and measured water. Bring to the boil, then lower the heat and simmer gently for 1 hour.

3 Remove from the heat and discard the ham bone. Season with pepper and salt, if necessary. Return the saucepan to the heat. Cook the remaining bacon in a hot frying pan until crisp, then add to the soup along with half the chives. Serve the soup in warmed bowls garnished with the remaining chives.

Green lentil and bacon soup

serves **6–8**
preparation time **15–20 minutes**
cooking time **1¼ hours**

25 g (1 oz) butter
125 g (4 oz) rindless smoked lean
   bacon, finely chopped
1 garlic clove, finely chopped
1 onion, finely chopped
425 g (14 oz) green lentils, rinsed
   and drained
1 celery stick, sliced
1 large carrot, diced
1 parsley sprig
1 thyme sprig or ¼ teaspoon
   dried thyme
1 bay leaf
1.2 litres (2 pints) Chicken Stock
   (see page 9)
900 ml (1½ pints) water
1 lemon slice
salt and pepper

1 Melt the butter in a large saucepan. Add the bacon, garlic and onion and cook over a moderate to high heat for 5 minutes, stirring constantly.

2 Lower the heat and add the lentils, celery, carrot, parsley, thyme and bay leaf to the pan. Pour in the stock and the measured water. Bring the mixture to the boil, skimming off the scum as it rises to the surface with a slotted spoon. Add the lemon slice.

3 Lower the heat, cover and simmer for 55–60 minutes, stirring occasionally. If the soup is too thick, stir in a little more water. Carefully remove and discard the parsley and thyme sprigs, bay leaf and lemon slice. Add salt and pepper to taste if necessary.

4 Measure 600 ml (1 pint) of the soup and purée it in a blender or food processor until smooth. Return the purée to the soup, stir well and cook over a moderate heat for 5 minutes. Serve in warmed soup bowls.

Turkey and vegetable soup

serves **8**

preparation time **25 minutes**

cooking time **about 2 hours**

1 large turkey drumstick, about
750 g (1½ lb)

2.4 litres (4 pints) water

1 small unpeeled onion, studded
with 4 cloves plus 1 large onion,
peeled and chopped

2 sprigs of parsley

1 bouquet garni

1 teaspoon salt

1 sprig of thyme, or ¼ teaspoon
dried thyme

1 sprig of marjoram, or ½ teaspoon
dried marjoram

3 carrots, chopped

2 celery sticks, sliced

250 g (8 oz) red lentils rinsed and
drained

250 g (8 oz) potatoes, peeled and
cut into 1 cm (½ inch) cubes

3 leeks, sliced

3 turnips, peeled and cut into 1 cm
(½ inch) cubes

2 tablespoons light soy sauce

pepper

3–4 tablespoons finely chopped
fresh parsley, to garnish

1 Place the drumstick in a large saucepan. Add the measured water, the studded onion, parsley sprigs, bouquet garni, salt, thyme and marjoram. Bring the mixture to the boil, lower the heat and simmer, partially covered, for 45 minutes.

2 Add the chopped onion, carrots and celery. Cook for 30 minutes over a low to moderate heat, then add the lentils, potatoes, leeks and turnips. Cook, until all the vegetables are tender. Remove the drumstick and let it cool. Remove and discard the bouquet garni, the studded onion with cloves and any parsley, thyme or marjoram stems.

3 Cut the turkey meat off the bone, discarding the skin. Carefully remove any small bones. Cut the meat into small pieces and return it to the saucepan. Add the soy sauce to the pan with pepper to taste. Heat the soup thoroughly and serve in a soup tureen, garnished with the parsley.

Cream of chicken soup

serves **6**
preparation time **15 minutes**
cooking time **1¼ hours**

1 chicken carcass
1 onion
1 bouquet garni
1 litre (2 pints) Chicken Stock
   (see page 9)
125 g (4 oz) cooked chicken
300 ml (½ pint) milk
50 g (2 oz) plain flour
2 tablespoons water
1 tablespoon lemon juice
¼ teaspoon grated nutmeg
salt and pepper

To garnish
croûtons (see page 18)
flat leaf parsley sprigs
grated nutmeg

To serve
150 ml (¼ pint) single cream
lemon wedges

1 Put the carcass, onion and bouquet garni into a saucepan with the stock. Simmer for about 1 hour. Strain the liquid and return it to the saucepan.

2 Neatly dice the cooked chicken meat and add to the stock with the milk. Blend the flour with the measured water, then slowly add the mixture to the stock, stirring constantly. Bring to the boil, then lower the heat and simmer gently for 10 minutes. Season the soup with lemon juice, nutmeg and salt and pepper to taste.

3 Pour the soup into warmed soup bowls, pour over the cream and garnish with croûtons, flat leaf parsley sprigs and some grated nutmeg. Serve with lemon wedges on the side.

Minestrone

serves **8–10**

preparation time **about 30 minutes**, plus soaking

cooking time **about 2¾ hours**

250 g (8 oz) dried haricot beans, soaked overnight in cold water to cover

3 tablespoons olive oil

2 onions, finely chopped

2 garlic cloves, finely chopped

2 rindless streaky bacon rashers, finely chopped

6 tomatoes, skinned and chopped

1.8 litres (3 pints) water

600 ml (1 pint) Beef Stock (see page 11)

1 courgette, diced

1 tablespoon chopped fresh marjoram or 1 teaspoon dried marjoram

1 teaspoon chopped fresh thyme or ½ teaspoon dried thyme

2 tablespoons tomato purée

2 carrots, diced

2 celery sticks, finely sliced

½ Savoy cabbage, finely shredded

250 g (8 oz) fresh shelled or frozen peas

50 g (2 oz) dried spaghetti, broken into small pieces or small pasta shapes

1 tablespoon chopped parsley

150 g (5 oz) grated Parmesan cheese

salt and pepper

1 Drain the beans thoroughly in a colander, then rinse under cold running water and drain again.

2 Heat the oil in a large saucepan, add the onions, garlic and bacon and cook over a moderate heat until the onions are transparent, but not brown, and the bacon is crisp.

3 Stir in the tomatoes, the measured water and stock, then add the courgette, beans, marjoram, thyme and tomato purée. Bring the mixture to the boil, skimming off the scum as it rises to the surface with a slotted spoon. Lower the heat and simmer, covered, for about 2 hours, or until the beans are tender.

4 Add the carrots and celery and cook over a moderate heat for a further 15 minutes, then add the cabbage, peas and pasta. Cook for 15–18 minutes, or until the vegetables and pasta are tender.

5 Add a little more water if the soup is too thick. Add the parsley, season to taste with salt and pepper and stir in 50 g (2 oz) of the Parmesan. Serve the soup immediately in warmed bowls, with the remaining Parmesan served separately.

Mulligatawny

serves **6–8**
preparation time **15–20 minutes**
cooking time **30–35 minutes**

1 onion, chopped
2 garlic cloves, chopped
2.5 cm (1 inch) piece of fresh root
   ginger, peeled and chopped
1/4 teaspoon cayenne pepper
1 teaspoon ground coriander
1/2 teaspoon ground cumin
1 teaspoon ground turmeric
4 teaspoons vegetable oil
3 boneless, skinless chicken
   breasts, halved
1.2 litres (2 pints) Chicken Stock
   (see page 9)
1.2 litres (2 pints) water
50 g (2 oz) long-grain white rice
125 g (4 oz) red lentils
1 tablespoon lemon juice
2 tablespoons grated creamed
   coconut
salt
6–8 lemon slices, to garnish

1 In a blender or food processor, purée the onion, garlic and ginger with the cayenne, coriander, cumin and turmeric to a smooth paste, scraping down the sides of the jug or bowl with a wooden or plastic spatula from time to time.

2 Heat the oil in a large saucepan and cook the onion paste over a moderate heat, stirring, for 2–3 minutes. Add the chicken breasts and cook, stirring, for a further 1–2 minutes.

3 Slowly pour in the stock and measured water, stirring constantly. Add the rice and lentils and simmer for 15–20 minutes, or until the rice is tender.

4 Remove the chicken, cut it into small pieces and set aside. Purée 900 ml (1 1/2 pints) of the soup mixture in a blender or food processor, then return it to the remaining soup in the pan. Add a little water if the soup is too thick and salt to taste.

5 Stir well, then add the lemon juice, coconut and reserved chicken pieces. Stir again and heat thoroughly without boiling for 3–5 minutes. Serve in warmed soup bowls, garnishing each portion with a lemon slice.

Bouillabaisse

serves **6–8**
preparation time **about
35 minutes**
cooking time **35–40 minutes**

4 tablespoons olive oil
2 garlic cloves, finely chopped
2 onions, chopped
500 g (1 lb) prepared mackerel,
   cut into chunks
500 g (1 lb) whiting fillet,
   cut into chunks
500 g (1 lb) haddock or cod fillet,
   cut into chunks
250 g (8 oz) raw prawns, peeled
6 tomatoes, skinned and chopped
1/2 teaspoon saffron threads
1.5 litres (2 1/2 pints) hot Fish Stock
   (see page 10)
1 bay leaf
3 parsley sprigs
10–12 live mussels, scrubbed and
   debearded
6–8 slices of French bread
salt and pepper
2 tablespoons finely chopped
   parsley, to garnish

1 Heat the oil in a large saucepan. Add the garlic and onions and cook, covered, for 3–5 minutes, or until the onions are transparent but not brown. Add the mackerel, whiting and haddock or cod and cook, uncovered, over a moderate heat for 10 minutes. Stir from time to time.

2 Add the prawns and tomatoes. Dissolve the saffron threads in the hot stock and add to the pan with the bay leaf, parsley sprigs and salt and pepper to taste. Stir and bring the mixture to the boil. Lower the heat and simmer, covered, for 15 minutes, then add the mussels and continue cooking for a further 10 minutes, or until the fish is cooked.

3 Remove and discard the bay leaf and parsley sprigs and any mussels that have not opened. Put the bread into a warmed soup tureen and ladle in the soup. Sprinkle with the chopped parsley before serving.

Clam chowder

serves **6–8**
preparation time **25–45 minutes**
cooking time **35–40 minutes**

48–60 live clams in closed shells
  (discard any that do not shut
  immediately when sharply
  tapped)
40 g (1½ oz) butter
125 g (4 oz) smoked streaky bacon,
  derinded and diced
2 large onions, finely chopped
2 celery sticks, diced
1–2 leeks, sliced
2 tablespoons finely chopped
  parsley, plus extra to garnish
2 bay leaves
leaves from 1 thyme sprig
900 ml (1½ pints) water
ground nutmeg
4–5 medium potatoes, diced
2 tablespoons plain flour
1–2 teaspoons, Worcestershire
  sauce
finely ground sea salt (optional)
  and pepper

1 Put the clams on a baking sheet in a preheated oven, 200°C (400°F), Gas Mark 6, for 2–3 minutes, or until they open slightly, then remove them and prise the shells apart. Open the shells over a bowl to catch all the clam juice. Snip off the inedible black-tipped necks (which resemble a tube), roughly chop the coral-coloured and pink flesh and leave the softer body meat whole.

2 Melt 25 g (1 oz) of the butter in a large saucepan. Add the bacon and cook for about 5 minutes, or until the fat starts to run. Add the onions, cover and cook gently for 10 minutes. Add the celery, leeks, parsley, bay leaves and thyme and cook for a further 5 minutes. Add the reserved clam juice, the measured water, nutmeg and pepper to taste and the potatoes. Stir well, taste and season with salt if necessary. Simmer gently for about 10 minutes, or until the potatoes are almost tender.

3 Meanwhile, cream the flour with the remaining butter to a smooth paste and reserve. Add the clams to the pan and simmer very gently for 3–4 minutes. Do not boil the soup or the clams will be tough and rubbery. Add a piece of the butter and flour paste to the pan, stirring well. When it has been fully incorporated, stir in a little more and continue until all the paste has been added. Stir for another 3–4 minutes, or until the soup thickens slightly.

4 Increase the heat briefly for 10 seconds, then remove from the heat. Add the Worcestershire sauce, stir and serve immediately in warmed soup bowls, garnished with parsley.

Prawn bisque

serves **4**
preparation time **20 minutes**
cooking time **35–45 minutes**

50 g (2 oz) butter
1 small carrot, finely chopped
½ small onion, finely chopped
½ celery stick, finely chopped
500 g (1 lb) raw prawns in their
   shells
250 ml (8 fl oz) dry white wine
2 tablespoons brandy
1.2 litres (2 pints) Fish Stock
   (see page 10)
1 bouquet garni
25 g (1 oz) long-grain white rice
100 ml (3½ fl oz) double cream
pinch of cayenne pepper
salt and pepper
4 tablespoons chopped parsley,
   to garnish

1 Melt the butter in a large heavy-based saucepan, add the carrot, onion and celery and cook, stirring occasionally, for 8–10 minutes, or until softened and lightly golden. Increase the heat, add the prawns and cook for 3–4 minutes, or until the shells turn pink all over.

2 Add the wine and brandy and bring to the boil, then lower the heat and simmer for 3–4 minutes, or until the prawns are cooked. Remove the prawns and leave to cool slightly. When cool enough to handle, peel the prawns, reserving the shells. Remove the black veins running down the back, chop the flesh and set aside.

3 Bring the liquid back to the boil and boil rapidly for 2–3 minutes, or until reduced by one-third. Add the reserved prawn shells with the stock, bouquet garni and rice. Bring to the boil, then lower the heat and simmer gently for 15–20 minutes, or until the rice is tender.

4 Remove and discard the bouquet garni. Purée the soup, including the shells, in a blender or food processor with three-quarters of the prawn meat. Strain through a fine sieve into a clean pan, pressing with the back of a ladle to push through as much liquid as you can. Add the cream and cayenne and season to taste with salt and pepper.

5 Bring the soup back to the boil, then lower the heat, add the reserved chopped prawns and cook for 1–2 minutes, or until heated through. Serve in warmed soup bowls, sprinkled with the chopped parsley.

Summer Soups

Whether warm or chilled, soup can be surprisingly refreshing on a hot summer's day. Packed with Mediterranean flavours, light ingredients and fragrant herbs, these elegant dishes are guaranteed to impress.

Chicory soup

serves **4**
preparation time **5 minutes**
cooking time **about 40 minutes**

75 g (3 oz) butter
1 onion, diced
2 chicory heads, finely chopped
50 ml (2 fl oz) dry white wine
1 litre (1¾ pints) milk
250 ml (8 fl oz) Vegetable or
   Chicken Stock (see pages 8
   and 9)
2 tablespoons cornflour
2 tablespoons grated Parmesan
   cheese
8 slices of stale bread, buttered
salt and pepper

1 Heat 50 g (2 oz) of the butter in a saucepan over a low heat, add the onion and cook until golden. Add the chicory and cook slowly in the butter for 10 minutes, then season to taste with salt and pepper. Pour in the wine, and when this has evaporated, stir in most of the milk and the stock. Bring slowly to the boil. Mix the cornflour with the remaining milk and add to the pan, stirring constantly to avoid lumps.

2 Cook for 25 minutes over a moderate heat, then whisk in the grated Parmesan and the remaining butter, cut into pieces.

3 Meanwhile, toast the stale bread in a preheated oven, 200°C (400°F), Gas Mark 6, for about 10 minutes, or until golden brown. Put the toast into warmed soup bowls and pour the soup over. Serve hot.

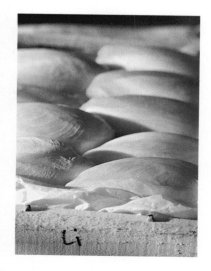

Celery, carrot and apple soup

serves **6**
preparation time **15 minutes**
cooking time **about 1 hour**

50 g (2 oz) unsalted butter
500 g (1 lb) celery, sliced
500 g (1 lb) carrots, chopped
250 g (8 oz) dessert apples, peeled,
   cored and roughly chopped
1.2 litres (2 pints) Vegetable Stock
   (see page 8)
1 teaspoon paprika
cayenne pepper, to taste
1 tablespoon chopped fresh basil
   leaves or 1 teaspoon dried basil
1 bay leaf
1 teaspoon freshly grated root
   ginger
salt and ground white pepper

To garnish
chopped celery leaves
paprika

1 Melt the butter in a large saucepan and add the celery, carrots and apple. Cover with a tight-fitting lid and cook over a low heat for 15 minutes, stirring occasionally.

2 Add the stock, paprika, cayenne, basil, bay leaf and ginger. Bring to the boil, then lower the heat and simmer, partially covered, for 40–45 minutes, or until the vegetables and apple are very soft.

3 Purée the mixture in a blender or food processor until smooth. Strain it through a sieve back into the pan and season to taste with salt and pepper. Reheat the soup. Serve the soup in warmed bowls, garnishing each portion with a few chopped celery leaves and a light sprinkling of paprika.

Jerusalem artichoke soup with artichoke crisps

serves **4**
preparation time **25 minutes**
cooking time **30 minutes**

1 small lemon
625 g (1¼ lb) Jerusalem artichokes
50 g (2 oz) butter
1 onion, chopped
1 garlic clove, crushed
1 celery stick, chopped
leaves from 1 lemon thyme sprig
1 litre (1¾ pints) Vegetable or
   Chicken Stock (see pages 8
   and 9)
vegetable oil, for deep-frying
175 ml (6 fl oz) single cream
   or milk
3 tablespoons finely grated
   Parmesan cheese
salt and pepper
flat leaf parsley leaves, to garnish

1 Finely grate the rind from the lemon and set it aside. Squeeze the juice and put it into a large bowl of cold water. Carefully peel the artichokes; reserve 2 and chop the rest into 1.5 cm (¾ inch) pieces, dropping them into the lemon water as you prepare them to prevent discoloration.

2 Melt the butter in a large saucepan, add the onion, garlic, celery, thyme and reserved lemon rind and cook gently, without allowing them to colour, for 6–8 minutes, or until softened. Drain the chopped artichokes and add to the pan with the stock. Season to taste with salt and pepper and bring to the boil. Lower the heat and simmer for about 15 minutes, or until the artichokes are tender.

3 To prepare the artichoke crisps, drain the 2 reserved whole artichokes, slice them thinly and dry well on kitchen paper. Heat some oil in a deep saucepan to 180–190°C (350–375°F), or until a cube of bread browns in 30 seconds. Add the artichoke slices in batches and fry until crisp and golden. Drain well on kitchen paper.

4 Purée the soup in a blender or food processor until smooth. Strain the soup through a sieve and return to the pan. Add the cream or milk, and a little water if too thick, season to taste and bring back to the boil. Stir in the finely grated Parmesan and serve in warmed bowls, sprinkled with the artichoke crisps and garnished with flat leaf parsley leaves.

Heart of artichoke soup with dill

serves **4–6**
preparation time **15–20 minutes**
cooking time **about 35 minutes**

50 g (2 oz) butter
1 onion, chopped
1 garlic clove, chopped
1 celery stick, sliced
425 g (14 oz) can artichoke hearts,
  drained
1.2 litres (2 pints) Vegetable or
  Chicken Stock (see pages 8
  and 9)
1 tablespoon lemon juice
3 tablespoons chopped dill
2 tablespoons plain flour
150 ml ($1/4$ pint) single cream
salt and ground white pepper
4–6 dill sprigs, to garnish

1 Melt the butter in a saucepan. Add the onion, garlic and celery and cook, covered, over a moderate heat for 10–12 minutes, or until all the vegetables are soft. Stir from time to time.

2 Add the artichoke hearts, replace the lid and cook for about a further 3 minutes. Pour in 1 litre ($1^3/4$ pints) of the stock and the lemon juice. Stir in 1 tablespoon of the dill, then cook, covered, over a moderate heat for 15 minutes.

3 Purée the mixture in a blender or food processor until smooth. Transfer to a clean saucepan.

4 Mix the flour with the remaining stock in a small bowl, adding a little water if necessary. Reheat the soup, whisk in the flour mixture and stir until the soup thickens slightly. Add the remaining dill, season to taste with salt and pepper, then add the cream. Heat thoroughly but do not allow the soup to boil or it will curdle. Serve in warmed soup bowls, garnished with dill sprigs.

Cream of sweetcorn soup

serves **4–6**
preparation time **5–10 minutes**
cooking time **about 30 minutes**

40 g (1½ oz) butter
1 onion, chopped
2 potatoes, diced
25 g (1 oz) plain flour
900 ml (1½ pints) milk
1 bay leaf
2 x 350 g (11½ oz) cans
   sweetcorn, drained
2 tablespoons double cream
salt and freshly ground
   white pepper
crumbled fried bacon, to garnish
garlic croûtons, to serve
   (see page 107)

1 Melt the butter in a large saucepan, add the onion and cook over a low heat, stirring frequently, for 5 minutes without browning. Add the potatoes and cook for a further 2 minutes.

2 Stir in the flour, then gradually add the milk, stirring constantly. Bring to the boil, add the bay leaf and season to taste with salt and pepper. Add half the sweetcorn, cover and simmer for 15–20 minutes.

3 Remove and discard the bay leaf and set the soup aside to cool slightly. Purée it in a blender or food processor until smooth. Return to the pan, add the remaining sweetcorn and heat through.

4 Stir in the cream, sprinkle over the bacon and serve the soup in warmed bowls with the garlic croûtons.

Fennel and lemon soup with black olive gremolata

serves **4**
preparation time **20 minutes**
cooking time **about 40 minutes**

75 ml (3 fl oz) olive oil
3 fat salad onions, chopped
250 g (8 oz) fennel, trimmed, cored
  and thinly sliced (reserve any
  green fronds for the gremolata)
1 potato, diced
finely grated rind and juice of
  1 lemon
750 ml (1¼ pints) Vegetable or
  Chicken Stock (see pages 8
  and 9)
salt and pepper

Black olive gremolata
1 small garlic clove, finely chopped
finely grated rind of 1 lemon
4 tablespoons chopped parsley
finely chopped green fronds from
  the fennel
16 Greek-style black olives, pitted
  and chopped

1 Heat the oil in a large saucepan, add the onions and cook for 5–10 minutes, or until beginning to soften. Add the fennel, potato and lemon rind and cook for 5 minutes. Pour in the stock and bring to the boil. Lower the heat, cover and simmer for about 25 minutes, or until the vegetables are tender.

2 Meanwhile, to make the gremolata, mix together the garlic, lemon rind, parsley and fennel fronds, then stir in the olives. Cover and chill in the refrigerator.

3 Purée the soup in a blender or food processor and pass it through a sieve to remove any strings of fennel. The soup should not be too thick, so add more stock if necessary. Return it to the rinsed-out pan. Taste and season well with salt, pepper and plenty of lemon juice. Pour into warmed soup bowls and sprinkle each serving with a portion of the gremolata, to be stirred in before eating.

Mint, cucumber and green pea soup

serves **6**
preparation time **15 minutes**,
plus chilling (if serving cold)
cooking time **25–30 minutes**

50 g (2 oz) butter
500 g (1 lb) cucumbers, peeled,
　deseeded and cut into 1 cm
　(½ inch) pieces
250 g (8 oz) shelled fresh or
　frozen peas
pinch of sugar
¼ teaspoon white pepper
3 tablespoons finely chopped mint
1.2 litres (2 pints) Vegetable or
　Chicken Stock (see pages 8
　and 9)
175 g (6 oz) potatoes, roughly
　chopped
150 ml (¼ pint) double cream
　(chilled, if the soup is to be
　served cold)
salt

1 Melt the butter in a large saucepan, add the cucumbers and cook over a moderate heat for 5 minutes, stirring occasionally. Add the peas, sugar, pepper and 2 tablespoons of the mint. Pour in the stock. Bring the mixture to the boil, then add the potatoes. Lower the heat and simmer, partially covered, for about 20 minutes, or until the potatoes are tender.

2 Purée the mixture in a blender or food processor until smooth. Transfer to a clean saucepan or, if the soup is to be served cold, to a bowl. Season to taste with salt.

3 If the soup is to be served hot, add the cream and reheat it gently without boiling. Serve in warmed bowls, garnishing each portion with a little of the remaining chopped mint. If the soup is to be served cold, cover the bowl closely and refrigerate for at least 3 hours. Just before serving, fold in the chilled cream. Serve in chilled bowls, garnished with the remaining chopped mint.

Roasted aubergine soup

serves **4–6**
preparation time **15 minutes**
cooking time **40–45 minutes**

1 kg (2 lb) aubergines
3 tablespoons olive oil
1 red onion
2 garlic cloves, crushed
1.2 litres (2 pints) Vegetable or
    Chicken Stock (see pages 8
    and 9)
200 ml (7 fl oz) crème fraîche or
    Greek yogurt
2 tablespoons chopped mint
salt and pepper
mint sprigs, to garnish

1 Put the aubergines under a preheated hot grill for about 20 minutes, turning occasionally, until the skin is well charred and the flesh has softened. Leave to cool slightly, then cut in half, scoop out the flesh and chop.

2 Heat the oil in a saucepan over a low heat, add the onion and garlic and cook gently, without colouring, for 5–6 minutes, or until softened. Add the chopped aubergine and the stock and cook for a further 10–15 minutes.

3 Purée the soup in a blender or food processor. Strain through a sieve and return to the pan to reheat. Season to taste with salt and pepper.

4 Mix the crème fraîche or Greek yogurt with the chopped mint and season to taste. Serve the soup in warmed bowls with a spoonful of the minted cream and garnish each serving with mint sprigs.

Bortsch

serves **6**
preparation time **15 minutes**
cooking time **about 1½ hours**

4 raw beetroot
4 tomatoes, skinned and chopped
1.2 litres (2 pints) Vegetable or
    Beef Stock (see pages 8 and 11)
3 large cabbage leaves, coarsely
    shredded
1 bay leaf
½ teaspoon caraway seeds
6 black peppercorns, crushed
5 tablespoons red wine vinegar
2 tablespoons sugar
6 small potatoes
salt
6 teaspoons soured cream,
    to garnish

1 Put the beetroot into a saucepan, cover with plenty of cold water and add 1 tablespoon salt. Bring to the boil, then lower the heat, cover and simmer for 35–45 minutes. Drain, discarding the liquid, then rinse the beetroot under cold water, dry with kitchen paper and slip off the skins.

2 Grate the beetroot into a large saucepan. Add the tomatoes, stock, cabbage leaves, bay leaf, caraway seeds, peppercorns, vinegar, sugar and 2 teaspoons salt. Stir well. Bring the mixture to the boil, then lower the heat, cover and simmer gently for about 30 minutes.

3 Remove and discard the bay leaf. Drop the potatoes into the soup and continue simmering until the potatoes are tender but not too soft. Serve the soup hot in warmed bowls, garnishing each portion with a teaspoon of soured cream.

Caldo verde

serves **6**
preparation time **15 minutes**
cooking time **40 minutes**

2 tablespoons olive oil
1 large onion, chopped
2 garlic cloves, chopped
500 g (1 lb) potatoes, cut into
   2.5 cm (1 inch) cubes
1.2 litres (2 pints) water or
   Vegetable Stock (see page 8)
250 g (8 oz) spring greens, finely
   shredded
2 tablespoons chopped parsley
salt and pepper
croûtons, to serve (see page 18),
   made with strips of bread
   instead of cubes

1 Heat the oil in a large frying pan, add the onion and cook for 5 minutes, or until softened but not brown. Add the garlic and potatoes and cook for a few minutes, stirring occasionally.

2 Transfer the vegetables to a large saucepan. Add the water or stock, season to taste with salt and pepper and cook for 15 minutes until the potatoes are tender.

3 Mash the potatoes roughly in their liquid, then add the spring greens and boil, uncovered, for 10 minutes.

4 Add the parsley and simmer for 2–3 minutes, or until heated through. Serve the soup in warmed bowls with croûtons.

Gazpacho

serves **6**

preparation time **10–15 minutes**,
plus chilling

2 garlic cloves, roughly chopped
¼ teaspoon salt
3 thick slices of white bread,
   crusts removed
1 kg (2 lb) tomatoes, skinned and
   roughly chopped
2 onions, roughly chopped
½ large cucumber, peeled,
   deseeded and roughly chopped
2 large green peppers, cored,
   deseeded and roughly chopped
5 tablespoons olive oil
4 tablespoons white wine vinegar
1 litre (1¾ pints) water
freshly ground black pepper

1 Combine the garlic and salt in a mortar and pound with a pestle until it is smooth. Put the bread into a bowl and cover it with cold water. Soak for 5 seconds, then drain the bread, squeezing out the moisture.

2 Set aside a quarter of the tomatoes, onions, cucumber and green peppers for the garnish. Put the remaining vegetables into a blender or food processor. Add the garlic paste, bread and oil and purée the mixture until smooth.

3 Pour the mixture into a bowl and stir in the vinegar and the measured water with pepper to taste. Cover closely and chill in the refrigerator for at least 3 hours.

4 Chop the reserved vegetables very finely and serve them separately in small bowls with the soup. Serve the soup very cold in chilled bowls.

Iced tomato and pepper soup with salsa verde

serves **4–6**

preparation time **about 30 minutes**, plus chilling

1 kg (2 lb) vine-ripened tomatoes, cored

2 large red peppers, cored, deseeded and roughly chopped

2 garlic cloves, chopped

1 small red chilli, deseeded and finely chopped

600 ml (1 pint) Mediterranean tomato juice or passata (sieved tomatoes)

6 tablespoons olive oil

2 tablespoons balsamic vinegar

salt and pepper

600 ml (1 pint) crushed ice, to serve

Salsa verde

2 garlic cloves, finely chopped

4 anchovy fillets in oil, rinsed and chopped

3 tablespoons each chopped parsley, mint and basil

2 tablespoons salted capers, rinsed and chopped

150 ml (¼ pint) olive oil, plus extra to seal

2 tablespoons lemon juice

1 Plunge the tomatoes into boiling water for 5–10 seconds, then remove them and refresh in cold water. Slip off the skins. Cut them in half around the middle and gently squeeze out and discard the seeds. Put the tomatoes into a blender or food processor.

2 Add the red peppers to the tomatoes with the garlic and chilli and blend to a rough purée. Transfer to a bowl and stir in the tomato juice or passata, oil and balsamic vinegar. Season with salt and pepper to taste, then cover and chill overnight in the refrigerator.

3 To make the salsa verde, pound 1 teaspoon salt with the garlic until creamy, using a pestle and mortar. Tip it into a bowl and stir in the anchovies, herbs, capers, oil, lemon juice and pepper to taste.

4 Stir the crushed ice into the soup and serve with the salsa verde in a separate bowl to stir into the soup.

Steamboat soup

serves **4–6**
preparation time **about
40 minutes**
cooking time **about 10 minutes**

8 tablespoons vegetable oil
10 garlic cloves, thinly sliced
1 tablespoon tamarind pulp
150 ml (¼ pint) boiling water
1.2 litres (2 pints) water
2 tablespoons Thai fish sauce
1 teaspoon caster sugar
1 small pineapple, peeled, cored
    and cut into chunks
175 g (6 oz) tomatoes, quartered
8 spring onions, finely sliced
250 g (8 oz) raw tiger prawns
3 squid, cleaned and cut into
    thick rings
250 g (8 oz) rainbow trout fillets,
    cut into pieces

To serve
handful of fresh coriander leaves
handful of basil leaves
2 large chillies, diagonally sliced

1 Heat the oil in a small saucepan and when it is hot deep-fry the garlic, a few slices at a time, until golden brown. Remove the garlic and drain on kitchen paper.

2 Put the tamarind pulp into a bowl with the measured boiling water and set aside for 20 minutes to soften and dissolve. Strain the liquid through a sieve (discarding the pods and tamarind stones) and put into a saucepan with the measured water, fish sauce, sugar, pineapple, tomatoes and spring onions. Slowly bring to the boil.

3 If you are using a steamboat, pour the flavoured stock into the hot pan containing smoking coals and add the tiger prawns, squid rings and pieces of fish. Simmer gently for 6–8 minutes. Alternatively, pour the hot stock into a large heavy-based saucepan, add the seafood and fish and simmer gently for 6–8 minutes, or until cooked and tender.

4 Serve the steamboat while the fish is still cooking, topped with coriander and basil leaves, slices of chilli and the deep-fried garlic.

Miso soup with tofu

serves **4**
preparation time **10 minutes**
cooking time **35–40 minutes**

2 tablespoons red or white miso
1 small leek, cut into fine julienne
    strips
125 g (4 oz) firm tofu, cut into
    small squares
1 tablespoon wakame seaweed

Dashi stock
15 g (½ oz) kombu seaweed
1.8 litres (3 pints) water
2 tablespoons dried tuna
    (bonito) flakes
chives, to serve

1 First make the dashi stock. Wipe the kombu seaweed with a damp cloth and put it into a saucepan with the measured water. Bring to a simmer, skimming off any scum that rises to the surface with a slotted spoon. When the soup is clear, add 1½ tablespoons of the dried tuna flakes and simmer, uncovered, for 20 minutes. Remove the pan from the heat and add the remaining dried tuna flakes. Set aside for 5 minutes, then strain the dashi and return it to the pan.

2 Mix the miso with a little of the warm stock, then add 1 tablespoon at a time to the stock, stirring all the time until the miso has dissolved. Remove from the heat until ready to serve.

3 Warm the miso soup and add the leek and tofu with the wakame seaweed.

4 To serve, blanch the chives, tie them into a bundle and float them on the top of the soup, then serve immediately in warmed bowls.

Mussel soup with saffron, basil and spinach

serves **4**
preparation time **30 minutes**
cooking time **about 20 minutes**

pinch of saffron threads
125 ml (4 fl oz) boiling water
750 g (1½ lb) live mussels,
   scrubbed and debearded
175 ml (6 fl oz) dry white wine
2 tablespoons olive oil
2 shallots, finely chopped
1 garlic clove, finely chopped
200 ml (7 fl oz) double cream
175 g (6 oz) young leaf spinach,
   trimmed
15 basil leaves, shredded

1 Put the saffron into a small heatproof bowl, pour over the measured boiling water and set aside to infuse. Discard any mussels that are broken or open. Put a large colander over another bowl.

2 Pour the wine into a saucepan large enough to accommodate all the mussels. Bring the wine to the boil and add the mussels. Cover with a tight-fitting lid and cook, shaking the pan frequently, for 2–3 minutes, or until the mussels have opened.

3 Tip the mussels into the colander and remove from their shells, discarding any that have not opened. Strain the mussel liquid through a muslin-lined sieve and set aside.

4 Heat the oil in a saucepan over a low heat, add the shallots and garlic and cook gently, without colouring, for 5–6 minutes, or until softened. Add the strained mussel liquid, cream and saffron and its infused liquid and bring to the boil. Lower the heat and add the spinach, half the basil and all the mussels. Simmer for 2 minutes, then remove from the heat, stir in the remaining basil and serve in warmed soup bowls.

Mediterranean salmon soup with rouille

serves **6**
preparation time **25 minutes**
cooking time **30 minutes**

1 tablespoon olive oil
25 g (1 oz) butter
1 onion, finely chopped
1 carrot, finely diced
1 potato, no more than 200 g
　(7 oz), diced
1 garlic clove, finely chopped
1 teaspoon paprika, plus extra
　to garnish
2 large pinches of saffron threads
2 tomatoes, skinned and diced
1 tablespoon tomato purée
900 ml (1½ pints) Fish Stock
　(see page 10)
125 ml (4 fl oz) dry white wine
2 salmon steaks, about 200 g
　(7 oz) each
150 ml (¼ pint) milk
150 ml (¼ pint) single cream
salt and pepper

Rouille
1 large mild red chilli, deseeded
　and chopped
1 garlic clove, finely chopped
3 tablespoons mayonnaise
1 small baguette, cut into 12 slices
　and toasted

1 Heat the oil and butter in a large saucepan, add the onion and cook gently for 5 minutes, stirring occasionally, until softened. Add the carrot and potato and cook for 5 minutes.

2 Stir in the garlic, paprika, saffron and tomatoes and cook for 1 minute. Add the tomato purée, stock and wine. Lower the salmon steaks into the stock and season generously with salt and pepper. Bring the stock to the boil, then lower the heat, cover and simmer for 10–12 minutes, or until the salmon flakes easily when pressed lightly with a knife.

3 Lift the salmon out of the pan, flake it into pieces using a knife and fork and discard the skin and bones. Reserve one quarter of the salmon for garnish, then return the rest to the pan and stir in the milk and cream. Purée the soup in a blender or food processor until smooth. Taste and adjust the seasoning if needed and reheat without boiling.

4 To make the rouille, purée the chilli, garlic and mayonnaise with a little salt and pepper in a blender or food processor until smooth. Toast the bread lightly on both sides and top with tiny spoonfuls of rouille. Ladle the soup into warmed bowls, sprinkle in the reserved salmon flakes and float the toasts on top. Sprinkle with paprika and serve immediately.

Lobster and sweetcorn chowder

serves **4**

preparation time **20 minutes**, plus
preparing the lobsters

cooking time **1 hour**

2 cooked lobsters, 750 g
  (1½ lb) each
25 g (1 oz) butter
1 onion, finely chopped
1 carrot, finely chopped
1 celery stick, finely chopped
1 thyme sprig
1 parsley sprig
2 bay leaves
1 litre (1¾ pints) water

Chowder

200 g (7 oz) can sweetcorn,
  drained
25 g (1 oz) butter
1 small onion, chopped
1 small garlic clove, crushed
50 g (2 oz) pancetta, cut into
  small strips
300 ml (½ pint) milk
300 ml (½ pint) single cream
1 kg (2 lb) potatoes, cut into
  1.5 cm (¾ inch) dice
cayenne pepper
4 tomatoes, skinned, deseeded
  and chopped
salt and pepper

1 Cut the lobsters in half lengthways and remove and discard the greyish-green tomalley (the liver), the gills and the intestinal vein running along the back. Smash the claws and remove the meat. Cut up the remaining meat. Put the shells into a polythene bag and smash into small pieces with a rolling pin.

2 Put the butter into a large saucepan and melt over a low heat. Add the onion, carrot and celery and cook for 8–10 minutes, or until soft.

3 Add the herbs, measured water and pieces of lobster shell. Bring to the boil, then lower the heat and simmer for 30 minutes. Strain through a fine sieve.

4 To make the chowder, place two-thirds of the sweetcorn in a blender or food processor with the strained lobster broth and purée until smooth. Melt the butter in a large flameproof casserole, add the onion and garlic and cook gently for 5 minutes.

5 Add the pancetta and cook until golden. Add the puréed sweetcorn mixture, the milk, cream, potatoes and remaining sweetcorn. Bring to the boil, then lower the heat and simmer for 10–15 minutes, or until the potatoes are tender.

6 Season to taste with cayenne, salt and pepper, then stir in the tomatoes and lobster meat. Heat through without boiling and serve in warmed soup bowls.

Hot and Spicy Soups

The robust flavours of a wealth of cuisines
are featured in these exotic recipes – sweet
and aromatic Middle Eastern; fragrant and
zesty Asian; piquant and fruity Caribbean;
and out-and-out fiery Mexican.

Roasted tomato and chilli soup with black olive cream

serves **4–6**
preparation time **30 minutes**
cooking time **about 1¼ hours**

1.5 kg (3 lb) ripe tomatoes,
   preferably plum
6 tablespoons olive oil
1½ teaspoons sea salt
1 tablespoon caster sugar
1 large red chilli
3–4 shallots or 1 onion, chopped
1 garlic clove, crushed
600 ml (1 pint) water
2–4 tablespoons lime juice
salt and pepper

Olive cream
50 g (2 oz) pitted black olives
50 g (2 oz) crème fraîche

1 Cut the tomatoes in half lengthways and, holding each half over a bowl, scoop out the seeds with a teaspoon. Reserve the tomato seeds and any juice.

2 Lightly grease a baking sheet with a little of the oil and lay the tomatoes on it, cut-side up. Sprinkle them with about 4 tablespoons of the remaining oil, the sea salt and sugar. Add the chilli and put the baking sheet in a preheated oven, 180°C (350°F), Gas Mark 4, for 45–50 minutes. Remove the chilli after 20 minutes, when it is well charred and blistered. When cool, peel, deseed and chop it roughly.

3 Meanwhile, to make the olive cream, chop the olives very finely, fold them into the crème fraîche and season to taste with salt and pepper.

4 Heat the remaining oil in a saucepan over a moderate heat, add the shallots or onion and cook for 6–8 minutes, or until lightly golden and softened. Add the garlic and cook for a further 2 minutes.

5 Add the roasted tomatoes with any liquid from the baking sheet, the reserved seeds and juice, the chilli and the measured water. Bring the soup to the boil, then lower the heat and simmer for 10–12 minutes.

6 Purée the soup in a blender or food processor. Strain through a sieve and return to the pan to reheat. Season to taste with salt, pepper and lime juice. Serve the soup in warmed bowls with a spoonful of the olive cream in each bowl.

Split pea soup with chorizo

serves **6–8**
preparation time **15–20 minutes**,
plus soaking
cooking time **about 2 hours**

375 g (12 oz) split yellow peas,
   soaked overnight in cold water
   to cover
2 tablespoons olive oil
3 chorizo sausages, thinly sliced
1 onion, chopped
2 garlic cloves, finely chopped
1.2 litres (2 pints) Chicken Stock
   (see page 9)
900 ml (1½ pints) water
1 bay leaf
1 thyme sprig or ¼ teaspoon
   dried thyme
3 carrots, quartered lengthways
   and thinly sliced
salt

1 Drain the soaked split peas in a colander, rinse under cold running water and drain again.

2 Heat the oil in a large saucepan. Cook the chorizo sausages over a moderate heat, stirring, for 5 minutes. With a slotted spoon, transfer the slices to kitchen paper to drain. Pour off all but 1 tablespoon of the fat in the pan.

3 Add the onion and garlic to the pan and cook over a moderate heat until softened. Add the drained split peas, stock, measured water, bay leaf and thyme. Bring the mixture to the boil, skimming off the scum as it rises to the surface with a slotted spoon. Lower the heat and simmer, partially covered, for 1¼ hours. Stir the mixture occasionally.

4 Add the carrots and cook for a further 30 minutes, or until tender. Season to taste with salt. Remove and discard the bay leaf, add the reserved chorizo and cook for a further 10 minutes. Serve in warmed soup bowls.

White bean soup
with toasted garlic and chilli oil

serves **6**

preparation time **35 minutes**, plus soaking

cooking time **1–1¼ hours**

250 g (8 oz) dried white beans (haricot, cannellini, etc.), soaked overnight in cold water to cover

Vegetable or Chicken Stock (see pages 8 and 9), or cold water, to cover

handful of sage leaves

4 garlic cloves

150 ml (¼ pint) olive oil

2 tablespoons chopped sage or rosemary

good pinch of chilli flakes

salt and pepper

roughly chopped parsley, to garnish

1 Drain the beans and put them into a flameproof casserole. Cover with the stock or water to a depth of 5 cm (2 inches) above the beans and push in the sage leaves. Bring the beans to the boil, then cover them tightly and bake in a preheated oven, 160°C (325°F), Gas Mark 3, for 40-60 minutes, depending on their freshness. Leave them in their cooking liquid.

2 Meanwhile, finely chop half the garlic and thinly slice the remainder.

3 Put half the beans, the cooked sage and all the liquid into a blender or food processor and blend until smooth. Pour the purée back into the casserole with the remaining beans. If the soup is thicker than liked, add extra water or stock to thin it.

4 Heat half the oil in a frying pan and add the chopped garlic. Cook gently until it is soft and golden, then add the chopped sage or rosemary and cook for 30 seconds. Stir the mixture into the soup and reheat until boiling. Simmer gently for 10 minutes. Taste and season well with salt and pepper. Pour into a warmed tureen or ladle into warmed soup bowls.

5 Cook the sliced garlic carefully in the remaining oil until golden (don't let it become too dark or it will be bitter), then stir in the chilli flakes. Dip the base of the pan into cold water to stop the garlic cooking, then spoon the garlic and oil over the soup. Serve sprinkled with chopped parsley.

Harira

serves **8–10**
preparation time **about
25 minutes**, plus soaking
cooking time **about 3 hours**

250 g (8 oz) chickpeas, soaked for
    48 hours in cold water to cover
    or 12 hours if covered with
    boiling water
2 chicken breasts, halved
1.2 litres (2 pints) Chicken Stock
    (see page 9)
1.2 litres (2 pints) water
2 x 425 g (14 oz) cans chopped
    tomatoes
¼ teaspoon crumbled saffron
    threads
2 onions, chopped
125 g (4 oz) long-grain white rice
50 g (2 oz) green lentils, rinsed
    and drained
2 tablespoons finely chopped fresh
    coriander
2 tablespoons finely chopped
    parsley
salt and pepper

1 Drain the chickpeas in a colander, rinse and drain again. Put them into a saucepan, cover with water to a depth of 5 cm (2 inches) above the chickpeas and bring to the boil. Lower the heat and simmer, partially covered, for 2 hours, or until the chickpeas are tender, adding more water as necessary. Drain and set aside.

2 Put the chicken breasts, stock and measured water in a separate saucepan. Bring to the boil, then lower the heat, cover and simmer for 10–15 minutes, or until the chicken is just cooked. Remove the chicken and shred it, discarding the skin and any bones. Set aside.

3 Add the chickpeas, tomatoes, saffron, onions, rice and lentils to the stock in the pan. Simmer, covered, for 30–35 minutes, or until the rice and lentils are tender.

4 Add the shredded chicken, coriander and parsley, and heat for 5 minutes without boiling. Season with salt and pepper and serve in warmed soup bowls.

Chilli bean and pepper soup

serves **6**
preparation time **20 minutes**
cooking time **40 minutes**

2 tablespoons sunflower oil
1 large onion, finely chopped
4 garlic cloves, finely chopped
2 red peppers, cored, deseeded
    and diced
2 red chillies, deseeded and finely
    chopped
900 ml (1½ pints) Vegetable Stock
    (see page 8)
750 ml (1¼ pints) tomato juice or
    passata (sieved tomatoes)
1 tablespoon double-concentrate
    tomato purée
1 tablespoon sun-dried tomato
    paste
2 tablespoons sweet chilli sauce,
    or more to taste
400 g (13 oz) can red kidney
    beans, drained
2 tablespoons finely chopped fresh
    coriander
salt and pepper
lime rind strips, to garnish
    (optional)

To serve
75 ml (3 fl oz) soured cream or
    crème fraîche
tortilla chips

1 Heat the oil in a large saucepan, add the onion and garlic and cook until soft but not coloured. Stir in the red peppers and chillies and fry for a few minutes. Stir in the stock and tomato juice or passata, tomato purée and paste, chilli sauce, beans and coriander. Bring to the boil, then lower the heat, cover and simmer for 30 minutes.

2 Cool slightly, then purée in a blender or food processor until smooth. Return the soup to the pan and taste and adjust the seasoning if necessary. Bring to the boil and serve in warmed soup bowls. Stir a little soured cream or crème fraîche into each portion and garnish with lime rind strips, if liked. Serve with tortilla chips.

Green lentil soup with spiced butter

serves **4**
preparation time **10 minutes**
cooking time **25–30 minutes**

2 tablespoons olive oil
2 onions, chopped
2 bay leaves
175 g (6 oz) green lentils, rinsed
    and drained
1 litre (1³/₄ pints) Vegetable Stock
    (see page 8)
¹/₂ teaspoon ground turmeric
small handful of fresh coriander
    leaves, roughly chopped
salt and pepper

Spiced butter
50 g (2 oz) lightly salted butter,
    softened
1 large garlic clove, crushed
1 tablespoon chopped fresh
    coriander
1 teaspoon paprika
1 teaspoon cumin seeds
1 red chilli, deseeded and finely
    chopped

1 Heat the oil in a large saucepan, add the onions and cook for 3 minutes. Add the bay leaves, lentils, stock and turmeric. Bring to the boil, then lower the heat, cover and simmer for 20 minutes, or until the lentils are tender and turning mushy.

2 Meanwhile, to make the spiced butter, beat the butter with the garlic, coriander, paprika, cumin and chilli and transfer the mixture to a small serving dish.

3 Stir the coriander leaves into the soup, season to taste with salt and pepper and serve in warmed soup bowls with the spiced butter in a separate bowl for stirring into the soup.

Red pepper and spicy chicken soup

serves **4**

preparation time **20 minutes**,
plus cooling

cooking time **50 minutes**

3 red peppers, halved, cored and
   deseeded

1 red onion, quartered

2 garlic cloves, unpeeled

2 teaspoons five-spice powder

150 g (5 oz) boneless, skinless
   chicken breast

1 teaspoon olive oil

5 cm (2 inch) piece of fresh root
   ginger, grated

1 teaspoon ground cumin

1 teaspoon ground coriander

1 large potato, chopped

900 ml (1½ pints) Chicken Stock
   (see page 9)

salt and pepper

4 tablespoons fromage frais,
   to serve

1 Place the peppers, onion and garlic cloves in a nonstick roasting tin. Roast in a preheated oven, 200°C (400°F), Gas Mark 6, for 40 minutes, or until the peppers have blistered and the onion quarters and garlic are very soft. If the onion quarters start to brown too much, cover them with the pepper halves.

2 Meanwhile, scatter the five-spice powder over the chicken breast and grill under a medium heat for 20 minutes until crisp. When cooked, cut the chicken into thin shreds and put aside.

3 While the chicken is grilling, heat the oil in a saucepan and fry the ginger, cumin and coriander over a low heat for 5 minutes, until softened. Add the potato and stir well, season and pour in the chicken stock. Simmer, covered, for 30 minutes.

4 Remove the cooked vegetables from the oven. Place the peppers in a polythene bag. Tie the top and leave to cool. (The steam produced in the bag makes it easier to remove the skin when cool.) Add the onions to the potato mixture and carefully squeeze out the garlic pulp into the saucepan, too. Peel the peppers and add to the soup. Simmer for 5 minutes.

5 Pour the soup into a blender or food processor and blend, in batches if necessary, for a few seconds until quite smooth. Return to the saucepan and thin with a little water, if necessary, to achieve the desired consistency. Stir the shredded chicken into the soup and simmer for 5 minutes.

6 Spoon into warmed bowls and top each one with a spoonful of fromage frais.

Spiced chickpea and lamb soup

serves **6**
preparation time **10 minutes**,
plus soaking
cooking time **2½ hours**

50 g (2 oz) chickpeas, soaked
   overnight in cold water to cover
50 g (2 oz) black-eyed beans,
   soaked overnight in cold water
   to cover
50 g (2 oz) trahana or bulgar
   wheat
500 g (1 lb) neck of lamb, cut into
   4 pieces
4 tablespoons olive oil
1 onion, chopped
2 carrots, chopped
425 g (14 oz) can chopped
   tomatoes
4 small red chillies
4 thyme sprigs
1 teaspoon each ground coriander,
   cumin and cinnamon
½ teaspoon each dried mint and
   oregano
salt and pepper

To serve
olive oil
crusty bread

1 Drain the soaked peas and beans in a colander, rinse under cold running water and drain again. Put them into separate saucepans, cover with plenty of cold water and bring to the boil. Lower the heat and simmer for 1 hour, then drain and reserve the liquid.

2 Place the cooked pulses in a clay pot or casserole dish, add all the remaining ingredients and cover with the reserved liquid, adding extra water to cover, if necessary.

3 Cover the casserole with a tight-fitting lid and bake in a preheated oven, 180°C (350°F), Gas Mark 4, for 1½ hours, or until the meat and vegetables are tender.

4 Serve each bowl of soup drizzled with olive oil and pass around some crusty bread.

Mexican soup with avocado salsa

serves **4**

preparation time **about
20 minutes**

cooking time **45 minutes**

2 tablespoons sunflower oil
1 large onion, chopped
2 garlic cloves, crushed
2 teaspoons ground coriander
1 teaspoon ground cumin
1 red pepper, cored, deseeded
   and diced
3 red chillies, deseeded and sliced
425 g (14 oz) can red kidney
   beans, drained and rinsed
750 ml (1¼ pints) tomato juice
1–2 tablespoons chilli sauce
25 g (1 oz) tortilla chips, crushed
salt and pepper
fresh coriander sprigs, to garnish

Avocado salsa
1 small ripe avocado
4 spring onions, finely chopped
1 tablespoon lemon juice
1 tablespoon chopped fresh
   coriander
salt and pepper

1 Heat the oil in a large saucepan. Add the onion, garlic, spices, red pepper and two-thirds of the chillies and cook gently for 10 minutes. Add the beans, tomato juice and chilli sauce. Bring to the boil, then lower the heat, cover and simmer gently for 30 minutes.

2 Meanwhile, to make the avocado salsa, peel, stone and finely dice the avocado. Put into a bowl and combine it with the spring onions, lemon juice and fresh coriander. Season to taste with salt and pepper, cover the bowl with clingfilm and set aside.

3 Purée the soup in a blender or food processor, together with the crushed tortilla chips. Return the soup to a clean saucepan, season with salt and pepper to taste and heat through. Serve immediately in warmed soup bowls with the avocado salsa. Garnish with the reserved chilli slices and the coriander sprigs.

Jamaican pepperpot soup

serves **6–8**
preparation time **30–35 minutes**
cooking time **about 1¼ hours**

1 kg (2 lb) lean stewing beef, cut
  into small cubes
250 g (8 oz) lean pork, cut into
  small cubes
2.5 litres (4 pints) water
24 okra, conical stalk end
  discarded and roughly chopped.
500 g (1 lb) kale, roughly chopped
500 g (1 lb) spinach, stems
  discarded and leaves roughly
  chopped
2 green peppers, cored, deseeded
  and roughly chopped
2 spring onions, roughly chopped
1 fresh thyme sprig or ¼ teaspoon
  dried thyme
¼ teaspoon cayenne pepper
500 g (1 lb) yellow yams, thinly
  sliced
1 large potato, thinly sliced
1 garlic clove, crushed or finely
  chopped
salt

1 Combine the meat with the measured water in a large saucepan. Bring to the boil, then lower the heat and simmer the meat, partially covered, for about 30 minutes.

2 Add the okra, kale, spinach, green peppers and spring onions to the pan with the thyme and cayenne. Cook over a moderate heat, partially covered, for 15 minutes.

3 Add the yams, potato and garlic to the pan and cook for a further 20 minutes, or until the yams and potato are soft. Add more water if the soup is too thick. Season to taste with salt. Serve the soup hot in a warmed soup tureen.

Callaloo

serves **6**
preparation time **15 minutes**
cooking time **35 minutes**

3 tablespoons groundnut oil
1 large onion, finely chopped
4 spring onions, finely chopped
2 garlic cloves, crushed
1 red chilli, deseeded and finely
   chopped
1 teaspoon turmeric
1 thyme sprig, crumbled
250 g (8 oz) okra, thinly sliced
500 g (1 lb) fresh callaloo or
   spinach leaves, hard stems
   discarded and roughly chopped
900 ml (1 1/2 pints) Vegetable or
   Chicken Stock (see pages 8
   and 9)
a few saffron threads
425 ml (14 fl oz) coconut milk
250 g (8 oz) crab meat, fresh or
   canned
juice of 1/2 lime
dash of hot pepper sauce
salt and pepper

1 Heat the oil in a large saucepan, add the onion, spring onions and garlic and cook gently for 5 minutes, or until softened. Add the chilli, turmeric and thyme and stir over a low heat for 1–2 minutes.

2 Stir in the okra, then add the callaloo or spinach leaves. Turn up the heat and cook, stirring, until the leaves start to wilt. Lower the heat and add the stock and saffron. Bring to the boil, then lower the heat, cover and simmer for 20 minutes.

3 Add the coconut milk and crab meat and stir well. Heat gently for 4–5 minutes and then season to taste with salt and pepper. Just before serving, stir in the lime juice and hot pepper sauce.

Moroccan fish soup

serves **6–8**
preparation time **about
35 minutes**
cooking time **about 40 minutes**

3 tablespoons olive oil
2 onions, chopped
2 celery sticks, sliced
4 garlic cloves, crushed
1 red chilli, deseeded and chopped
$\frac{1}{2}$ teaspoon ground cumin
1 cinnamon stick
$\frac{1}{2}$ teaspoon ground coriander
2 large potatoes, chopped
1.5 litres (2$\frac{1}{2}$ pints) Fish Stock
   (see page 10) or water
3 tablespoons lemon juice
2 kg (4 lb) mixed fish and shellfish,
   prepared
4 well-flavoured tomatoes,
   skinned, deseeded if liked and
   chopped
1 large bunch of mixed dill, parsley
   and fresh coriander, chopped
salt and pepper

1 Heat the oil in a large saucepan. Add the onion and celery and cook gently until softened and transparent, adding the garlic and chilli towards the end. Add the cumin, cinnamon and ground coriander and stir for 1 minute, then add the potatoes and cook, stirring, for a further 2 minutes.

2 Add the stock or water and the lemon juice and simmer gently, uncovered, for about 20 minutes, or until the potatoes are tender.

3 Add the fish and shellfish, the tomatoes, herbs and salt and pepper to taste and cook gently until the fish and shellfish are tender. Serve in warmed soup bowls.

tip Any selection of fish and shellfish can be used for fish soup, with the exception of oily fish such as mackerel and sardines. The trimmings, heads, tails, bones and shells can be used to make the fish stock.

Wonton soup

serves **4**
preparation time **25 minutes**
cooking time **15 minutes**

20 wonton wrappers
1.2 litres (2 pints) Chicken Stock
  (see page 9)
2 pink Asian shallots or 1 small
  onion, finely chopped
2.5 cm (1 inch) piece of fresh root
  ginger, peeled and finely sliced
1 teaspoon caster sugar
4 spring onions, finely sliced
1/2 tablespoon light soy sauce
1 teaspoon rice vinegar
handful of roughly chopped parsley
1 teaspoon sesame oil
salt and pepper
chilli oil, to serve

Filling
125 g (4 oz) white fish or prawns
125 g (4 oz) white crab meat
2 spring onions, finely chopped
2.5 cm (1 inch) piece of fresh
  root ginger, peeled and
  finely chopped
1 garlic clove, crushed

1 First make the filling. Chop the fish or prawns and crab meat very finely with the spring onions, chopped ginger and garlic or put all the ingredients in a blender or food processor and blend to a paste.

2 Put 1 teaspoon of the mixture on a wonton wrapper, brush around the filling with a little water and fold the wrapper over to make a triangle. Repeat with the remaining mixture until all the wontons are made. Keep the wrappers covered with a damp cloth to prevent them from drying out before you fill them.

3 Put the stock into a saucepan with the shallots or small onion and sliced ginger and bring to the boil. Lower the heat and add the sugar and filled wontons. Simmer gently for 5 minutes.

4 Add the spring onions, soy sauce, vinegar, parsley and salt and pepper to taste. Just before serving, add the sesame oil. Serve the soup in warmed bowls accompanied by small dishes of chilli oil.

Hot and sour prawn noodle soup

serves **4**
preparation time **20 minutes**,
plus soaking
cooking time **35–40 minutes**

500 g (1 lb) raw large prawns in
   their shells, defrosted if frozen
1 tablespoon sunflower oil
2 spring onions, roughly chopped
2.5 cm (1 inch) piece of fresh root
   ginger, peeled and chopped
1 small red or green chilli,
   deseeded and finely chopped
2 Kaffir lime leaves or rind from
   1 lime, cut into strips
2 lemon grass stalks, bruised and
   chopped into 2.5 cm (1 inch)
   pieces, or 1 tablespoon dried
   chopped lemon grass, soaked
   in hot water to cover for
   30 minutes
1.2 litres (2 pints) Chicken Stock
   (see page 9)
2–4 tablespoons lime juice
75 g (3 oz) fine egg or rice noodles
125 g (4 oz) small oyster
   mushrooms

To garnish
2 spring onions, cut into thin strips
fresh coriander sprigs

1 Peel and devein the prawns, reserving the shells. Rinse the prawns and set aside.

2 Heat the oil in a large saucepan, add the chopped spring onions, ginger and chilli and cook gently, without colouring, for 5 minutes. Add the reserved prawn shells and cook for 3 minutes, then add the lime leaves or rind, lemon grass (if using dried lemon grass, add it with its soaking liquid), stock and 2 tablespoons lime juice. Bring to the boil, then lower the heat and simmer gently for 20 minutes.

3 Meanwhile, cook the noodles according to the packet instructions, drain and set aside.

4 Strain the stock through a fine sieve into a clean pan. Taste and add more lime juice if required. Bring back to the boil, then lower the heat, add the prawns and cook for about 2 minutes, or until opaque. Add the mushrooms and cook for 1–2 minutes, or until just soft. Add the noodles and heat through. Serve in warmed soup bowls, sprinkled with spring onion strips and coriander sprigs.

Malaysian laksa

serves **4**
preparation time **15 minutes**
cooking time **25–30 minutes**

3 tablespoons groundnut oil
2 large onions, finely chopped
4 garlic cloves, crushed
3 red bird's eye chillies, finely
    chopped
75 g (3 oz) roasted peanuts,
    chopped
1 tablespoon ground coriander
1 tablespoon ground cumin
2 teaspoons turmeric
1.2 litres (2 pints) coconut milk
1 teaspoon shrimp paste
1–2 tablespoons sugar, to taste
375 g (12 oz) cooked chicken,
    shredded
175 g (6 oz) bean sprouts
500 g (1 lb) fresh flat rice noodles
4 spring onions, chopped
3 tablespoons chopped fresh
    coriander leaves
salt and pepper

To serve
4 spring onions, chopped
1 large red chilli, finely sliced
1–2 tablespoons chopped roasted
    peanuts

1 Heat the oil in a saucepan, add the onions and cook until golden brown. Add the garlic, chillies, peanuts, ground coriander, cumin and turmeric and cook for 2–3 minutes, or until the spices have cooked through and released a strong aroma.

2 Stir the coconut milk and shrimp paste into the spice mixture, cover and simmer for 15 minutes. Season the spiced coconut with salt, pepper and sugar to taste. Add the shredded chicken and half the bean sprouts and simmer for 5 minutes.

3 Blanch the noodles in boiling water and divide between 4 large bowls. Sprinkle with the spring onions and fresh coriander and divide the remaining raw bean sprouts between the bowls.

4 Ladle the chicken and coconut mixture over the noodles and serve with spring onions, red chilli and roasted peanuts, in separate bowls for garnishing.

Beef and flat noodle soup

serves **4–6**
preparation time **25 minutes**
cooking time **2¼ hours**

500 g (1 lb) chuck steak
1.8 litres (3 pints) Beef Stock
   (see page 11) or water
4 star anise
1 large cinnamon stick
1 teaspoon black peppercorns
2 sweet onions or 4 shallots,
   thinly sliced
4 garlic cloves, crushed
7 cm (3 inch) piece of fresh root
   ginger, finely sliced
125 g (4 oz) bean sprouts
250 g (8 oz) dried flat rice noodles
6 spring onions, thinly sliced
handful of fresh coriander leaves
250 g (8 oz) fillet of beef, thinly
   sliced
2 tablespoons fish sauce
salt and pepper
red bird's eye chillies, to garnish

Nuoc cham sauce
2 red chillies, chopped
1 garlic clove
1½ tablespoons caster sugar
1 tablespoon lime juice
1 tablespoon rice vinegar
3 tablespoons fish sauce
4 tablespoons water

To serve
bean sprouts
thin spring onions, sliced
1 large red chilli, sliced

1 Heat a large dry frying pan until very hot and sear the chuck steak on all sides until brown and charred.

2 Put the beef into a large saucepan with the stock or water, star anise, cinnamon, black peppercorns, 1 sliced onion or 2 shallots, the garlic and ginger. Bring to the boil, skimming off any scum that rises to the surface with a slotted spoon, and continue to boil for about 10 minutes. Lower the heat, cover and simmer for about 2 hours, or until the beef is tender.

3 Blanch the bean sprouts in boiling water for 1 minute.

4 Cook the noodles in boiling water for 3–4 minutes, or until just soft. Do not overcook them. Drain well and put into 4 large soup bowls. Arrange the bean sprouts, spring onions, coriander leaves and the remaining onions or shallots over the noodles.

5 To make the nuoc cham sauce, pound the chopped chillies, garlic and sugar until smooth, using a pestle and mortar. Add the lime juice, vinegar, fish sauce and measured water and blend together well. Put the mixture into a small bowl.

6 When the beef from the broth is tender, lift it out, slice it thinly and divide it between the soup bowls with the slices of raw fillet and garnish with the red bird's eye chillies.

7 Strain the broth, return it to the pan and season to taste with fish sauce, salt and pepper. To serve, ladle the hot broth over the contents of the bowls and serve immediately with the nuoc cham sauce and a plate of extra bean sprouts, spring onions and red chilli.

Winter Warmers

The perfect meal-in-a-bowl, there is nothing more comforting and satisfying than soup. These hearty dishes are thick with root vegetables, pulses and grains, and include delicious toppings, such as garlic croûtons, grated cheese or soured cream.

Cream of celeriac soup with porcini dumplings

serves **4–6**
preparation time **25 minutes**,
plus soaking and chilling
cooking time **35–40 minutes**

50 g (2 oz) butter
2 shallots or 1 onion, chopped
1 garlic clove, crushed
500 g (1 lb) celeriac, cut into
  small dice
900 ml (1½ pints) Vegetable or
  Chicken Stock (see pages 8
  and 9)
300 ml (½ pint) single cream
  or milk
salt and pepper
finely grated Parmesan cheese,
  to serve

Dumplings
5 g (¼ oz) dried porcini
  mushrooms (ceps)
25 g (1 oz) butter
1 shallot, finely chopped
175 g (6 oz) ricotta cheese
25 g (1 oz) finely grated Parmesan
  cheese
2 egg yolks, beaten
2 tablespoons plain flour, plus
  extra for rolling
1 tablespoon chopped parsley

1 To make the dumplings, put the porcini into a small bowl and pour over warm water to cover. Leave to soak for 30 minutes. Drain in a fine sieve, reserving the liquid. Rinse the mushrooms well in cold water, chop finely and set aside.

2 Melt the butter in a small saucepan over a low heat, add the shallot and cook gently, without colouring, for 5–6 minutes, or until softened. Spoon into a bowl, add the remaining ingredients and mix to form a soft dough. Season to taste with salt and pepper. Cover and refrigerate for 30–60 minutes. With lightly floured hands, form the mixture into about 30 small balls, roll in flour and put on to a tray.

3 Meanwhile, to make the soup, melt the butter in a saucepan over a moderate heat, add the shallots or onion and garlic and cook, without colouring, for 5 minutes. Add the celeriac, cover and cook for 5–10 minutes, or until the celeriac begins to soften. Add the stock and bring to the boil, then lower the heat and simmer for 10–15 minutes.

4 Purée the soup in a blender or food processor until smooth. Return the soup to the pan, stir in the cream or milk and season to taste. Reheat without boiling.

5 Bring a saucepan of lightly salted water to the boil. Add the dumplings and simmer for 3–4 minutes. Drain well and add to the soup just before serving. Serve in warmed soup bowls, sprinkled with grated Parmesan.

Chestnut soup

serves **6**

preparation time **20 minutes**, plus soaking (if using dried chestnuts)

cooking time **45 minutes–1 hour**

750 g (1½ lb) fresh, plump, sweet chestnuts or 400 g (13 oz) dried chestnuts, soaked overnight in cold water to cover
125 g (4 oz) butter
150 g (5 oz) pancetta or streaky bacon, chopped
2 onions, finely chopped
1 carrot, chopped
1 celery stick, chopped
2 garlic cloves, halved
1 tablespoon chopped rosemary
2 bay leaves
salt and pepper
rosemary sprigs, to garnish

1 If you are using fresh chestnuts, use a small sharp knife to slit the shell of each chestnut across the rounded side. Put them into a saucepan and cover with cold water. Bring to the boil, then lower the heat and simmer for 15–20 minutes. Lift out the chestnuts and discard the water. Peel off the thick outer skin and the thinner inner skin, which has a bitter taste.

2 Melt the butter in a large saucepan and add the pancetta or bacon. Cook over a moderate heat until beginning to turn golden. Add the onions, carrot and celery and cook for 5–10 minutes, or until softened.

3 Add the chestnuts to the pan (including the soaking water from dried chestnuts) with the garlic, rosemary and bay leaves and enough water to cover completely. Bring to the boil then simmer for 30 minutes, stirring occasionally. Season with salt and pepper. Serve in warmed bowls, garnished with rosemary.

Sweet potato soup

serves **6–8**
preparation time **15 minutes**
cooking time **50 minutes–1 hour**

4–6 rindless smoked bacon rashers
25 g (1 oz) butter
1 onion, chopped
2 carrots, sliced
2 celery sticks, sliced
1 bay leaf
750 g (1½ lb) sweet potatoes,
   sliced
250 g (8 oz) potatoes, sliced
1.2 litres (2 pints) Chicken Stock
   (see page 9)
150 ml (¼ pint) water
125 ml (4 fl oz) dry white wine
¼ teaspoon grated nutmeg
¼ teaspoon white pepper
salt

1 Heat the bacon in a frying pan over a gentle heat until the fat runs, then raise the heat and cook over a moderate heat until very crisp. Using tongs, transfer the bacon on to kitchen paper to drain.

2 Add the butter to the bacon fat left in the frying pan and cook the onion, carrots, celery and bay leaf over a low heat for 5–8 minutes, stirring frequently.

3 Transfer the mixture to a saucepan. Add the sweet potatoes, potatoes, stock, measured water and wine. Bring the mixture to the boil, then lower the heat and simmer, covered, for 35–40 minutes, or until the vegetables are very tender. Remove and discard the bay leaf.

4 Purée the mixture in a blender or food processor until smooth. Transfer to a clean saucepan. Add the nutmeg, white pepper and salt to taste. Put the pan over a moderate heat, stirring, until the soup is hot.

5 Serve the soup in warmed bowls, garnishing each portion with the reserved bacon.

Tomato and bread soup

serves **4**
preparation time **10 minutes**
cooking time **about 35 minutes**

1 kg (2 lb) vine-ripened tomatoes,
   skinned, deseeded and chopped
300 ml (½ pint) Vegetable Stock
   (see page 8)
6 tablespoons olive oil
2 garlic cloves, crushed
1 teaspoon sugar
2 tablespoons chopped basil
100 g (3⅓ oz) day-old bread,
   without crusts
1 tablespoon balsamic vinegar
salt and pepper
pesto, to serve (optional)

1 Put the tomatoes into a saucepan with the stock, 2 tablespoons of the oil, the garlic, sugar and basil and bring gradually to the boil. Lower the heat, cover and simmer gently for 30 minutes.

2 Crumble the bread into the soup and stir over a low heat until it has thickened. Stir in the balsamic vinegar and the remaining oil and season to taste with salt and pepper. Stir a spoonful of pesto into each bowl before serving, if liked.

Kale soup with garlic croûtons

serves **8–10**
preparation time **20–25 minutes**
cooking time **about 45 minutes**

50 g (2 oz) butter
1 onion, chopped
2 carrots, sliced
500 g (1 lb kale), thick stems
   discarded
1.2 litres (2 pints) water
600 ml (1 pint) Vegetable Stock
   (see page 8)
1 tablespoon lemon juice
300 g (10 oz) potatoes, sliced
pinch of grated nutmeg
salt and pepper
2 kale leaves, finely shredded,
   to garnish
garlic croûtons, to serve
   (see below)

1 Melt the butter in a large saucepan, add the onion and cook over a moderate heat until soft but not brown, stirring frequently. Add the carrots and kale in batches, stirring constantly. Cook for 2 minutes. Add the measured water, stock, lemon juice, potatoes, nutmeg and salt and pepper to taste. Bring to the boil, stirring from time to time. Lower the heat, cover and simmer for 30–35 minutes, or until all the vegetables are soft.

2 Purée the mixture in a blender or food processor until smooth. Transfer to a clean pan. If it is too thick, add some water.

3 Add the shredded kale leaves to the pan and cook, stirring constantly, until crisp.

4 Check the seasoning and reheat the soup without boiling. Serve in warmed soup bowls with the garlic croûtons and garnish with the crisp kale.

tip To make garlic croûtons, cut the crusts off 2 slices of white bread and gently rub the bread all over with the cut sides of a halved garlic clove, then cube the bread. Heat 1 tablespoon vegetable oil in a heavy-based frying pan and fry the bread cubes, turning and stirring frequently, for 1–2 minutes, or until golden and crisp.

Pumpkin and apple soup

serves **4–5**
preparation time **15 minutes**
cooking time **30 minutes**

2 tablespoons butter
1 large onion, roughly chopped
2 teaspoons chopped fresh thyme
2 small cooking apples, peeled,
  cored and roughly chopped
3 tablespoons dark soft brown
  sugar
2 tablespoons whole-grain
  mustard
1 small pumpkin, about 750 g
  (1½ lb), skinned, deseeded and
  cut into chunks
1 litre (1¾ pints) Vegetable Stock
  (see page 8)
125 g (4 oz) crème fraîche
salt and pepper
pumpkin seeds, to serve

1 Melt the butter in a large saucepan. Add the onion and thyme and cook gently, stirring frequently, for about 5 minutes, or until softened and beginning to colour. Add the apples and sugar and cook gently for a further 3 minutes.

2 Add the mustard, pumpkin and stock and bring just to the boil. Lower the heat, cover and simmer gently for about 20 minutes, or until the pumpkin and apples are very soft and falling apart.

3 Purée the mixture in a blender or food processor until smooth.

4 Stir in half the crème fraîche, season to taste with salt and pepper and heat through gently. Ladle into warmed soup bowls, spoon over the remaining crème fraîche and serve sprinkled with pumpkin seeds.

Oven-baked vegetable soup

serves **4**
preparation time **15 minutes**
cooking time **about 1¼ hours**

1 onion, roughly chopped
2 garlic cloves, chopped
2 large carrots, thinly sliced
1 leek, thickly sliced
1 large parsnip, diced
175 g (6 oz) swede, diced
4 tablespoons olive oil
2 teaspoons clear honey
4 thyme sprigs
4 rosemary sprigs
2 bay leaves
4 ripe tomatoes, quartered
1.2 litres (2 pints) Vegetable Stock
    (see page 8)
salt and pepper
buttered toast, to serve

1 Toss the vegetables with the oil and honey and put into a roasting tin. Add the herbs and transfer to a preheated oven, 200°C (400°F), Gas Mark 6. Roast for about 50–60 minutes, or until all the vegetables are golden and tender. Add the tomatoes halfway through cooking. Lower the oven temperature to 190°C (375°F), Gas Mark 5.

2 Remove and discard the herbs and transfer the vegetables to a blender or food processor. Add half the stock and process until smooth, then blend in the remaining stock.

3 Transfer the soup to a casserole dish, season to taste with salt and pepper and bake for 20 minutes, or until heated through. Serve in warmed soup bowls with buttered toast.

Country bean and vegetable broth

serves **4**

preparation time **10 minutes**, plus soaking

cooking time **about 1¼ hours**

25 g (1 oz) each dried kidney beans, pinto beans and black-eyed beans, soaked overnight in cold water to cover, drained and rinsed

25 g (1 oz) dried porcini mushrooms (ceps)

1 tablespoon olive oil

2 shallots, finely chopped

2 garlic cloves, crushed

125 g (4 oz) button mushrooms, diced

2 tablespoons chopped mixed fresh herbs, plus extra to garnish

50 g (2 oz) mini pasta shapes

1.2 litres (2 pints) hot Beef Stock (see page 11)

salt and pepper

1 Put the beans into a large saucepan with water to cover. Bring to the boil and boil vigorously for 10 minutes. Skim any scum that rises to the surface of the liquid with a slotted spoon and lower the heat. Simmer, covered, for 1 hour, or until all the beans are very tender.

2 Meanwhile, put the dried mushrooms into a heatproof bowl, cover with boiling water and set aside for 15 minutes, then drain and reserve the liquid.

3 Heat the oil in a large saucepan, add the shallots and garlic and cook for 3 minutes. Add the fresh mushrooms and stir well. Add the herbs and pasta shapes. Drain the beans and add them to the saucepan with the hot stock, reserved mushroom liquid and salt and pepper to taste. Bring to the boil, then lower the heat and simmer for about 12 minutes. Serve immediately in warmed bowls, sprinkled with chopped herbs to garnish.

Tasty bean soup

serves **4**
preparation time **30 minutes**,
plus soaking
cooking time **about 2¼ hours**

375 g (12 oz) dried haricot beans,
   soaked overnight in cold water
   to cover
2 litres (3½ pints water)
1 carrot, chopped
1 onion, quartered
1 bouquet garni
125 g (4 oz) cooked smoked ham,
   diced
40 g (1½ oz) butter
2 shallots, finely chopped
1 garlic clove, crushed
1 tablespoon chopped parsley
salt and pepper
parsley sprigs, to garnish
125 g (4 oz) croûtons, to serve
   (see page 18)

1 Drain the beans in a colander, rinse under cold running water and drain again.

2 Put the beans into a large saucepan with the measured water and bring to the boil over a moderate heat. Boil for 1½ hours, or until the beans are just tender. Add the carrot, onion, bouquet garni and ham and simmer for 20–30 minutes. Remove and discard the bouquet garni. Purée the soup in a blender or food processor until smooth. Return to the pan and reheat over a moderate heat.

3 Melt the butter in a heavy-based saucepan, add the shallots and garlic and cook gently until golden but not brown. Add the parsley and mix together quickly. Add the shallot mixture to the bean purée.

4 Mix well with a wooden spoon, season well with salt and pepper, then pour into warmed soup bowls. Sprinkle with croûtons and garnish with parsley sprigs.

Goulash soup

serves **6–8**
preparation time **10–15 minutes**
cooking time **1¼ hours**

3 tablespoons vegetable oil
750 g (1½ lb) boneless lean beef,
   cut into 2.5 cm (1 inch) strips
2 onions, chopped
2 garlic cloves, crushed
2 celery sticks, sliced
3 tablespoons paprika
1 tablespoon caraway seeds
1.2 litres (2 pints) Beef Stock
   (see page 11)
600 ml (1 pint) water
¼ teaspoon dried thyme
2 bay leaves
¼ teaspoon Tabasco sauce,
   or to taste
3 tablespoons tomato purée
250 g (8 oz) potatoes, cut into
   1 cm (½ inch) dice
3 carrots, cut into 1 cm (½ inch)
   dice
6–8 teaspoons soured cream,
   to garnish (optional)

1 Heat the oil in a large saucepan and brown the meat in batches over a moderate heat. As each batch browns, transfer it to kitchen paper to drain. Add the onions, garlic and celery to the remaining oil and cook until transparent.

2 Take the pan off the heat and stir in the paprika, caraway seeds, stock and the measured water. Add the thyme, bay leaves, Tabasco and tomato purée. Stir well and add the cooked beef. Bring the mixture to the boil, then lower the heat and simmer, partially covered, for 30 minutes.

3 Add the diced potatoes and carrots, then simmer for a further 30 minutes, or until the potatoes are tender. Remove and discard the bay leaves. Serve the soup immediately in warmed bowls, garnishing each portion with a teaspoon of soured cream, if liked.

Spanish chickpea soup

serves **8–10**
preparation time **15 minutes**,
plus soaking
cooking time **2½–2¾ hours**

150 g (5 oz) dried chickpeas,
  soaked for 48 hours in cold
  water to cover or 12 hours if
  covered with boiling water
1 small smoked, boneless bacon
  hock joint, about 500–750 g
  (1–1½ lb)
1 onion, studded with 4 cloves
2 garlic cloves, crushed
1 bay leaf
1 thyme sprig or ¼ teaspoon
  dried thyme
1 marjoram sprig or ½ teaspoon
  dried marjoram
1 parsley sprig
1.8 litres (3 pints) water
1.8 litres (3 pints) Chicken Stock
  (see page 9)
300–375 g (10–12 oz) potatoes,
  cut into 1 cm (½ inch) dice
300 g (10 oz) Savoy cabbage,
  shredded
salt and pepper

1 Drain the chickpeas in a colander, rinse under cold running water and drain again. Put the bacon joint into a deep saucepan and cover with cold water. Bring the water briefly to the boil, then drain, discarding the water.

2 Return the bacon joint to the clean saucepan. Add the chickpeas, onion, garlic, bay leaf, thyme, marjoram, parsley and the measured water. Bring the mixture to the boil, then lower the heat and simmer, partially covered, for 1½ hours. Remove and discard the onion, bay leaf and thyme, marjoram and parsley sprigs. Lift out the hock, put it on a board and cut it into small pieces. Set the pieces aside.

3 Add the stock, potatoes and cabbage to the pan and simmer for a further 30 minutes. Add the reserved hock pieces to the soup and cook for a further 10 minutes. Season to taste with salt and pepper. Serve in warmed soup bowls.

La Ribollita

serves **8**

preparation time **30 minutes**, plus soaking and chilling

cooking time **about 3 hours**

150 ml (¼ pint) olive oil

1 onion, finely chopped

1 carrot, chopped

1 celery stick, chopped

2 leeks, finely chopped

4 garlic cloves, finely chopped

1 small white cabbage, shredded

1 large potato, chopped

4 courgettes, chopped

200 g (7 oz) dried cannellini beans, soaked overnight in cold water to cover, drained and rinsed

400 g (13 oz) passata (sieved tomatoes)

2 rosemary sprigs

2 thyme sprigs

2 sage sprigs

1 dried red chilli

2 litres (3½ pints) water

500 g (1 lb) cavolo nero (Tuscan black cabbage) or Savoy cabbage, finely shredded

6 thick slices of coarse crusty white bread

1 garlic clove, bruised

salt and pepper

To serve

olive oil

freshly grated Parmesan cheese

1 Heat half the oil in a large saucepan and add the onion, carrot and celery. Cook gently for about 10 minutes, stirring frequently. Add the leeks and finely chopped garlic and cook for a further 10 minutes. Add the white cabbage, potato and courgettes, stir well and cook for a further 10 minutes, stirring frequently.

2 Stir in the soaked beans, passata, rosemary, thyme and sage, dried chilli, salt to taste and plenty of black pepper. Cover with the measured water (the vegetables should be well covered) and bring to the boil, then lower the heat and simmer, covered, for at least 2 hours, or until the beans are very soft.

3 Remove 2–3 ladlefuls of soup, mash it well, then return to the pan. Stir in the cavolo nero or Savoy cabbage and simmer for a further 15 minutes. Leave the soup to cool, then cover and refrigerate overnight.

4 The next day, slowly reheat the soup, season if necessary and stir in the remaining oil. Toast the bread and rub it with the bruised garlic. Arrange the bread over the base of a tureen or in individual bowls and ladle the soup over it. Drizzle with oil and serve with plenty of freshly grated Parmesan.

Risi e bisi with frazzled prosciutto

serves **4**
preparation time **10 minutes**
cooking time **20–30 minutes**,
plus **5–10 minutes** for fresh peas

750 g (1½ lb) fresh young peas in
  the pod, shelled, or 250 g (8 oz)
  frozen peas, defrosted
3 tablespoons olive oil
1 onion, chopped
1.2 litres (2 pints) Chicken Stock
  (see page 9)
200 g (7 oz) risotto rice
large pinch of sugar
4 slices of prosciutto
2 tablespoons chopped flat leaf
  parsley
50 g (2 oz) Parmesan cheese, finely
  grated, plus extra to serve
salt and pepper

1 Heat 2 tablespoons of the oil in a large saucepan, add the onion and cook, without colouring, for 5–10 minutes, or until softened.

2 Add the stock and bring to the boil, then lower the heat and stir in the rice. (If using fresh peas, add them now and simmer gently for 5 minutes before adding the rice.) Season with salt and pepper and add the sugar. Cover and simmer gently, stirring occasionally, for 15–20 minutes, or until the rice is just tender. (If using frozen peas, add them after 10–15 minutes.)

3 Cut each slice of prosciutto in half lengthways. Heat the remaining oil in a large frying pan, add the prosciutto strips and cook over a high heat for 10–15 seconds, or until crisp. Drain on kitchen paper.

4 Stir the parsley and grated Parmesan into the soup. Serve in warmed soup bowls, topped with 2 pieces of the frazzled prosciutto and some grated Parmesan.

Barley soup with pork and cabbage

serves **6**
preparation time **15 minutes**
cooking time **55 minutes**

4 tablespoons olive oil
1 garlic clove, chopped
1 onion, chopped
1.2 litres (2 pints) Beef Stock
    (see page 11)
750 ml (1 1/4 pints) water
300 g (10 oz) lean pork, cut into
    1.5 cm (3/4 inch) strips
2 carrots, chopped
300 g (10 oz) spring or Savoy
    cabbage, roughly chopped
125 g (4 oz) pearl barley
300 g (10 oz) potatoes, cut into
    1 cm (1/2 inch) dice
salt and pepper

1 Heat the oil in a large saucepan, add the garlic and onion and cook over a moderate heat until softened.

2 Add the stock, the measured water, pork, carrots, cabbage and barley. Bring the mixture to the boil, then lower the heat, cover and simmer for 20 minutes.

3 Add the potatoes with salt and pepper to taste. If the soup is too thick, add a little water. Replace the lid and simmer for a further 30 minutes. Stir from time to time. Serve in warmed soup bowls.

Gruyère soup with bacon and potatoes

serves **6–8**
preparation time **20 minutes**
cooking time **about 25 minutes**

2 tablespoons olive oil
3 rindless smoked bacon rashers,
   chopped
2 onions, finely chopped
600 ml (1 pint) Chicken Stock
   (see page 9)
900 ml (1½ pints) water
625 g (1¼ lb) potatoes, cut into
   1 cm (½ inch) dice
4 tablespoons plain flour
50 g (2 oz) Gruyère cheese, grated
1 tablespoon medium dry sherry
1 teaspoon Worcestershire sauce
3 tablespoons finely chopped
   parsley
salt and pepper

1 Heat the oil in a large saucepan, add the bacon and onions and cook over a moderate heat until the onion is pale golden. Add the stock, 600 ml (1 pint) of the measured water and the potatoes. Bring the mixture to the boil, then lower the heat, cover and simmer, for 15 minutes, or until the potatoes are just tender.

2 In a small bowl, whisk the flour with the remaining water and stir it into the soup. Cook, covered, for 5 minutes, stirring frequently.

3 Blend the Gruyère with 300 ml (½ pint) of the soup in a blender or food processor. Stir the purée back into the soup, then add the sherry and Worcestershire sauce with salt and pepper to taste. Simmer for 3–5 minutes, then stir in the parsley just before serving in warmed soup bowls.

Smoked haddock and sweetcorn soup with wild rice and bacon croûtons

serves **4**

preparation time **15 minutes**

cooking time **about 1¼ hours**

75 g (3 oz) wild rice

250 g (8 oz) smoked haddock

600 ml (1 pint) milk

1 bay leaf

50 g (2 oz) butter

1 large onion, chopped

1 leek, sliced

1 celery stick, chopped

1 garlic clove, crushed

1 tablespoon thyme leaves

900 ml (1½ pints) Chicken Stock
    (see page 9)

pinch of grated nutmeg

125 g (4 oz) sweetcorn, defrosted
    if frozen

salt and pepper

2 tablespoons chopped parsley,
    to serve

Bacon croûtons

3 tablespoons olive oil

4 rindless pancetta slices or
    streaky bacon rashers,
    cut into strips

2 slices of bread, crusts removed,
    cut or broken into 1 cm (½ inch)
    pieces

1 Put the rice into a small saucepan and cover with cold water. Bring to the boil, then lower the heat and simmer for 40–45 minutes, or until tender. Drain and set aside.

2 Put the haddock, milk and bay leaf into a saucepan and bring to the boil, then lower the heat and simmer for 8–10 minutes, or until just cooked. Remove the fish with a slotted spoon and leave to cool. Discard the skin and any bones and break the flesh into flakes with a fork. Strain the milk and reserve it.

3 Melt the butter in a large saucepan, add the onion, leek, celery and garlic and cook, without colouring, for 8–10 minutes. Add the thyme, stock and reserved milk. Season with salt, pepper and nutmeg. Bring to the boil, then lower the heat and simmer for 10 minutes. Add the sweetcorn and cook for 5 minutes, then add the rice and flaked haddock and heat for a few minutes. Adjust the seasoning to taste.

4 To make the bacon croûtons, heat the oil in a large frying pan over a moderate heat, add the pancetta or bacon and cook for 5–6 minutes, or until crisp.

5 Remove with a slotted spoon and drain on kitchen paper. Add the bread to the pan and cook for 4–5 minutes, turning frequently, until crisp and golden brown. Drain on kitchen paper.

6 Serve the soup in warmed soup bowls, sprinkled with the bacon croûtons and chopped parsley.

Eight treasure soup

serves **4–6**
preparation time **15–20 minutes**
cooking time **about 15 minutes**

1.2 litres (2 pints) Chicken Stock
  (see page 9) or water
50 g (2 oz) frozen peas
50 g (2 oz) frozen sweetcorn
1 small boneless, skinless chicken
  breast, about 100 g (3½ oz), cut
  into very thin strips
75 g (3 oz) fresh shiitake
  mushrooms, stalks removed,
  very thinly sliced
3 tablespoons soy sauce,
  or to taste
2 tablespoons rice wine or
  dry sherry
1 tablespoon cornflour
50 g (2 oz) cooked peeled prawns,
  defrosted and dried thoroughly
  if frozen
50 g (2 oz) cooked ham, thinly
  sliced
150 g (5 oz) firm tofu, drained and
  thinly sliced
50 g (2 oz) fresh baby spinach
  leaves, very finely shredded
salt and pepper

1 Bring the stock or water to the boil in a large saucepan. Add the frozen peas and sweetcorn and simmer for 3 minutes. Add the chicken, mushrooms, soy sauce and rice wine or sherry. Stir well and simmer for 3 minutes.

2 Blend the cornflour to a paste with a little cold water, then pour into the soup and stir to mix. Simmer, stirring, for 1–2 minutes, or until the soup thickens.

3 Lower the heat to low and add the prawns, ham, tofu and spinach. Simmer for about 2 minutes, or until the spinach is just wilted, stirring once or twice. Take care to stir gently so that the tofu does not break up. Taste and add salt and pepper if necessary, plus more soy sauce, if liked. Serve piping hot.

Wheat noodle soup with marinated chicken

serves **4–6**

preparation time **30 minutes**,
plus marinating

cooking time **20–25 minutes**

300 g (10 oz) boneless, skinless
  chicken breasts
1 teaspoon turmeric
2 teaspoons salt
2 lemon grass stalks
3 tablespoons peanuts, skinned
  and roasted
3 tablespoons long-grain
  white rice
2 tablespoons vegetable oil
1 onion, chopped
3 garlic cloves, crushed
5 cm (2 inch) piece of fresh root
  ginger, peeled and finely
  chopped
1/4 teaspoon paprika
2 red bird's eye chillies, chopped
2–3 tablespoons Thai fish sauce
900 ml (1½ pints) water
250 g (8 oz) wheat noodles

To serve
3 hard-boiled eggs, halved
2 tablespoons chopped fresh
  coriander leaves
3 spring onions, finely chopped
Thai fish sauce
crushed dried chilli
1–2 tablespoons balachaung
  (optional)

1 Cut the chicken breasts into 2.5 cm (1 inch) cubes.
Mix the turmeric with the salt and rub it into the
cubes of chicken. Cover and leave to stand for
30 minutes.

2 Bruise the lemon grass with the side of a rolling pin
to release the flavour. Finely crush the roasted peanuts
in a food processor or using a pestle and mortar. Heat
a dry frying pan and toast the rice until golden brown,
then finely crush it to a powder in a food processor or
spice grinder.

3 Heat the oil in a large saucepan, add the onion and
cook until just softened. Add the dry marinated chicken
together with the lemon grass, garlic, ginger, paprika
and chillies. Add the fish sauce and measured water
and bring to the boil.

4 Lower the heat and simmer gently. Mix the crushed
peanuts and ground rice and add to the pan. Simmer
for 10–15 minutes, or until the chicken has cooked
through and the broth thickened slightly.

5 Meanwhile, bring a saucepan of water to the boil,
add the noodles and cook for 3–4 minutes, or until just
tender. Drain and refresh with cold water, then divide
between large soup bowls.

6 Ladle the chicken soup over the noodles and serve
topped with hard-boiled eggs, chopped coriander and
spring onions. Add an extra splash of fish sauce and a
sprinkling of crushed dried chilli and balachaung, if
using, to taste. Eat the soup with a spoon and fork.

tip Balachaung is a hot Burmese condiment made
from deep-fried shallots, garlic, chillies and dried
shrimps. You can just use deep-fried shallots, which,
like balachaung, are available from Oriental shops.

Index

A

anchovies, iced tomato and pepper with salsa verde 67
apples
celery, carrot and apple soup 55
pumpkin and apple soup 108–9
artichokes
heart of artichoke soup with dill 58
Jerusalem artichoke soup with artichoke crisps 56–7
Asian-style soups 6
beef and flat noodle 98–9
chicken and coconut milk 28
eight treasure 123
garnishes 7
hot and sour prawn noodle 95
Malaysian laksa 96–7
miso soup with tofu 70
pork ball and tofu 29
prawn and lemon grass 30–1
steamboat 68–9
wheat noodle soup with marinated chicken 124–5
wonton 94
aubergines, roasted aubergine soup 62
avgolemono 6, 25
avocados, Mexican soup with avocado salsa 88–9

B

bacon
chestnut soup 103
green lentil and bacon soup 43
Gruyère soup with bacon and potatoes 120–1
mushroom soup with crispy bacon 40
smoked haddock and sweetcorn soup with wild rice and bacon croûtons 122
Spanish chickpea soup 115
sweet potato soup 104–5
see also ham
barley soup with pork and cabbage 119
basil
mussel soup with saffron, basil and spinach 71
tomato and bread soup 106
bean sprouts
beef and flat noodle soup 98–9
Malaysian laksa 96–7
prawn and lemon grass soup 30–1
beans
chilli bean and pepper soup 82
country bean and vegetable broth 111
minestrone 46–7
la ribollita 116–17
tasty bean soup 112–13
white bean soup with toasted garlic and chilli oil 80–1
beef
beef and flat noodle soup 98–9
goulash soup 114
Jamaican pepperpot soup 90
beef stock 11
beetroot, bortsch 63
black pepper cream, roasted pepper soup with 36–7
bortsch 6, 63
bouillabaisse 49
bread
French onion soup 41
Mediterranean salmon soup with rouille 72–3
la ribollita 116–17
tomato and bread soup 106
see also croûtons
broccoli
broccoli and cheese soup 14–15
spinach and broccoli soup 22–3
butter, green lentil soup with spiced butter 84–5

C

cabbage
barley soup with pork and 119
bortsch 63
la ribollita 116–17
Spanish chickpea soup 115
caldo verde 64–5
callaloo 91
carrots
carrot and ginger soup 17
celery, carrot and apple soup 55
goulash soup 114
oven-baked vegetable soup 110
la ribollita 116–17
celeriac, cream of celeriac soup with porcini dumplings 102
celery
celery, carrot and apple soup 55
la ribollita 116–17
cheese
broccoli and cheese soup 14–15
French onion soup 41
Gruyère soup with bacon and potatoes 120–1
spinach and broccoli soup 22–3
see also Parmesan cheese
chestnut soup 103
chicken
and coconut milk soup 28
cream of chicken soup 45
eight treasure soup 123
harira 82
Malaysian laksa 96–7
red pepper and spicy chicken soup 86
stock 9
wheat noodle soup with marinated chicken 124–5
chickpeas
harira 82
Spanish chickpea soup 115
spiced chickpea and lamb soup 87
chicory soup 54
chillies
chilli bean and pepper soup 82
roasted tomato and chilli soup with black olive cream 78
white bean soup with toasted garlic and chilli oil 80–1

chorizo, split pea soup with 79
clam chowder 50
coconut milk
callaloo 91
chicken and coconut milk soup 28
Malaysian laksa 96–7
cold soups
gazpacho 66
iced tomato and pepper with salsa verde 67
mint, cucumber and green pea soup 61
courgettes
courgette and mint soup 20
la ribollita 116–17
crab
callaloo 91
soup 26–7
wonton soup 94
cream of celeriac soup with porcini dumplings 102
cream of chicken soup 45
cream of sweetcorn soup 59
croûtons 7
caldo verde 64–5
kale soup with garlic croûtons 107
making 18
pea, lettuce and lemon soup with sesame croûtons 21
smoked haddock and sweetcorn soup with wild rice and bacon croûtons 122
tasty bean soup 112–13
tomato soup with 34
cucumber
gazpacho 66
mint, cucumber and green pea soup 61

D

dill, heart of artichoke soup with 58

E

eggs
watercress soup with poached quails' eggs 24
wheat noodle soup with marinated chicken 124–5

F

fennel
fennel and lemon

soup with black olive gremolata 60
parsnip and fennel soup 16
finishing touches 7
fish and seafood
bouillabaisse 49
clam chowder 50
lobster and sweetcorn chowder 74–5
Mediterranean salmon soup with rouille 72–3
Moroccan fish soup 92–3
smoked haddock and sweetcorn soup with wild rice and bacon croûtons 122
steamboat soup 68–9
fish stock 10
freezing
soups 7
stock 6
French onion soup 41

G
garlic
Jamaican pepperpot soup 90
kale soup with garlic croûtons 107
oven-baked vegetable soup 110
la ribollita 116–17
white bean soup with toasted garlic and chilli oil 80–1
garnishes 7
gazpacho 66
ginger, carrot and ginger soup 17
globe artichokes, heart of artichoke soup with dill 58
goulash soup 6, 114
Greece 6
green lentil and bacon soup 43
green lentil soup with spiced butter 84–5
Gruyère soup with bacon and potatoes 120–1

H
ham
eight treasure soup 123
risi e bisi with frazzled prosciutto 118
tasty bean soup 112–13
see also bacon
ham and pea soup 42
harira 6, 82

hot and sour prawn noodle soup 95

I
iced tomato and pepper with salsa verde 67

J
Jamaican pepperpot soup 90
Jerusalem artichoke soup with artichoke crisps 56–7

K
kale
Jamaican pepperpot soup 90
kale soup with garlic croûtons 107

L
la ribollita 116–17
laksa, Malaysian 96–7
lamb, spiced chickpea and lamb soup 87
leeks
leek and potato soup 39
oven-baked vegetable soup 110
la ribollita 116–17
Vichyssoise 38
lemon
avgolemono 25
fennel and lemon soup with black olive gremolata 60
pea, lettuce and lemon soup with sesame croûtons 21
lemon grass
hot and sour prawn noodle soup 95
prawn and lemon grass soup 30–1
wheat noodle soup with marinated chicken 124–5
lentils
green lentil and bacon soup 43
green lentil soup with spiced butter 84–5
harira 82
mulligatawny 48
lettuce, pea, lettuce and lemon soup with sesame croûtons 21
lobster and sweetcorn chowder 74–5

M
Malaysian laksa 96–7
Mediterranean salmon soup with rouille 72–3

Mexican soup with avocado salsa 88–9
minestrone 46–7
mint
courgette and mint soup 20
mint, cucumber and green pea soup 61
roasted aubergine soup 62
miso soup with tofu 70
Moroccan fish soup 92–3
Morocco 6
mulligatawny 6, 48
mushrooms
country bean and vegetable broth 111
cream of celeriac soup with porcini dumplings 102
eight treasure soup 123
mushroom soup with crispy bacon 40
mussels
bouillabaisse 49
mussel soup with saffron, basil and spinach 71

N
noodles
beef and flat noodle soup 98–9
hot and sour prawn noodle soup 95
Malaysian laksa 96–7
wheat noodle soup with marinated chicken 124–5
nuoc cham sauce, beef and flat noodle soup 98–9

O
okra
callaloo 91
Jamaican pepperpot soup 90
olives
fennel and lemon soup with black olive gremolata 60
roasted tomato and chilli soup with black olive cream 78
onions, French onion soup 41
oven-baked vegetable soup 110

P
pancetta, chestnut soup 103
Parmesan cheese

chicory soup 54
Jerusalem artichoke soup with artichoke crisps 56–7
la ribollita 116–17
risi e bisi with frazzled prosciutto 118
parsley, potato soup with 18–19
parsnips
oven-baked vegetable soup 110
parsnip and fennel soup 16
pasta
country bean and vegetable broth 111
minestrone 46–7
pea, lettuce and lemon soup with sesame croûtons 21
peanuts, Malaysian laksa 96–7
pearl barley, barley soup with pork and cabbage 119
peas
eight treasure soup 123
mint, cucumber and green pea soup 61
risi e bisi with frazzled prosciutto 118
see also split peas
peppers
chilli bean and pepper soup 82
gazpacho 66
iced tomato and pepper with salsa verde 67
Jamaican pepperpot soup 90
Mexican soup with avocado salsa 88–9
red pepper and spicy chicken soup 86
roasted pepper soup with black pepper cream 36–7
porcini mushrooms
country bean and vegetable broth 111
cream of celeriac soup with porcini dumplings 102
pork
barley soup with pork and cabbage 119
Jamaican pepperpot soup 90
pork ball and tofu soup 29
potatoes
caldo verde 64–5

goulash soup 114
Gruyère soup with
bacon and potatoes
120–1
Jamaican pepperpot
soup 90
leek and potato soup
39
potato soup with
parsley 18–19
la ribollita 116–17
Spanish chickpea soup
115
Vichyssoise 38
prawns
bouillabaisse 49
eight treasure soup
123
prawn bisque 51
prawn and lemon
grass soup 30–1
steamboat soup 68–9
wonton soup 94
prosciutto, risi e bisi with
frazzled prosciutto
118
pulses, canned 7
pumpkins
pumpkin and apple
soup 108–9
pumpkin soup 35

Q
quail's eggs, watercress
soup with poached
quails' eggs 24

R
rice
avgolemono 25
harira 82
mulligatawny 48
prawn bisque 51
risi e bisi with frazzled
prosciutto 6, 118
rice noodles
beef and flat noodle
soup 98–9
Malaysian laksa 96–7
risi e bisi with frazzled
prosciutto 6, 118

roasted aubergine soup
62
rouille, Mediterranean
salmon soup with
72–3
Russia 6

S
salmon, Mediterranean
salmon soup with
rouille 72–3
salsa
iced tomato and
pepper with salsa
verde 67
Mexican soup with
avocado salsa 88–9
Savoy cabbage
la ribollita 116–17
Spanish chickpea soup
115
seafood see fish and
seafood
sesame croûtons, pea,
lettuce and lemon
soup with 21
smoked haddock and
sweetcorn soup
with wild rice and
bacon croûtons
122
spices 7
spinach
and broccoli soup
22–3
callaloo 91
eight treasure soup
123
Jamaican pepperpot
soup 90
mussel soup with
saffron, basil and
spinach 71
split peas
ham and pea soup 42
split pea soup with
chorizo 79
spring greens, caldo
verde 64–5
squid, steamboat soup
68–9

stock 6, 8–11
beef 11
chicken 9
fish 10
freezing 6
fresh supermarket
stock 6
stock cubes and
powders 6
vegetable 8
swede, oven-baked
vegetable soup 110
sweet potato soup 104–5
sweetcorn
cream of sweetcorn
soup 59
eight treasure soup
123
lobster and sweetcorn
chowder 74–5
smoked haddock and
sweetcorn soup
with wild rice and
bacon croûtons
122

T
tasty bean soup 112–13
time-savers 6–7
tofu
eight treasure soup
123
miso soup with 70
pork ball and tofu
soup 29
tomatoes
chilli bean and pepper
soup 82
gazpacho 66
harira 82
iced tomato and
pepper with salsa
verde 67
Mediterranean salmon
soup with rouille
72–3
minestrone 46–7
Moroccan fish soup
92–3
la ribollita 116–17
roasted tomato and

chilli soup with
black olive cream
78
tomato and bread
soup 106
tomato soup with
croûtons 34
turkey and vegetable
soup 44

V
vegetables
country bean and
vegetable broth
111
minestrone 46–7
oven-baked vegetable
soup 110
la ribollita 116–17
turkey and vegetable
soup 44
vegetable stock 8
Vichyssoise 38
Vietnamese soups 6

W
watercress soup with
poached quails'
eggs 24
white bean soup with
toasted garlic and
chilli oil 80–1
wild rice, smoked
haddock and
sweetcorn soup
with wild rice and
bacon croûtons
122
wonton soup 94

Y
yams, Jamaican
pepperpot soup 90

Acknowledgements

Executive Editor: Nicky Hill
Senior Editor: Rachel Lawrence
Executive Art Editor: Leigh Jones
Designer: Tony Truscott
Picture Researcher: Luzia Strohmayer
Production Controller: Manjit Sihra

Octopus Publishing Group Limited /Frank Adam 8, 110 /Stephen
Conroy 100–101, 109 /David Loftus 93 /Jeremy Hopley 39 /David
Jordan 73 /Sandra Lane 28, 54, 51–52, 57 /William Lingwood 21 /David
Loftus 2, 22, 50, 69, 94, 97, 99, 118, 125 /Diana Miller 35, 66, 90, 107,
115 /Peter Myers 7, 11, 17, 62 /Sean Myers 32–33, 41, 83, 89 /William
Reavell 24, 43, 45, 82, 85, 111, 113, 119 /Simon Smith 47, 59 /Ian
Wallace 3, 4, 15, 25, 27, 31, 37, 60, 67, 71, 76, 78, 81, 87, 103, 106,
117, 123 /Philip Webb 1, 12–13, 19, 49, 65, 75, 105, 121.